Living to Serve

By Jan Black
Designed and Illustrated by Steve Hunt and Dave Adamson

We, the people who made this book,
like to help kids serve others and God.

And the one who helped all of us was God,
who wants even more than we do
to help you learn to serve.

purposeful design®
p u b l i c a t i o n s
A Division of ACSI

Books, Textbooks, and Educational Resources
for Christian Educators and Schools Worldwide

Purposeful Design Publications is the publishing division of ACSI and is committed to the ministry of Christian school education, to enable Christian educators and schools worldwide to effectively prepare students for life. As the publisher of books, textbooks, and other educational resources within ACSI, Purposeful Design Publications strives to produce biblically sound materials that reflect Christian scholarship and stewardship and that address the identified needs of Christian schools around the world.

Character Foundation Series—*Living to Serve*
Student Edition—Sixth Grade
ISBN 1-58331-152-1 **Catalog** #7037

Association of Christian Schools International
PO Box 65130 • Colorado Springs, CO 80962-5130
Customer Service: 800.367.0798 • www.acsi.org

Table of Contents

Living To Serve

Living To Serve

THE IDEA

Here is an idea that may sound odd to you: Serve others and you will find the secret of happiness. The reason it may sound odd is that it has been changed around to sound like this: Serve yourself and you will find the secret of happiness.

The first idea is the one that came from the mind of God. The second idea came from the mind of people. It is up to you to choose whose mind to trust.

THE BOOK

This book takes God's idea of serving others and explores it. It helps you see how serving others is done and gives you ways to try it yourself.

In the book, you will meet a woman who served her country, some kids who serve all kinds of people, and the true God who serves the universe.

THE PLAN

By looking at the Table of Contents you can see how the book is organized. By looking at the titles of the units, you can see the ways of serving that you will be studying. The servant stories were planned for you by students your age. They had fun swapping good ideas and thinking of you.

Some people live to eat. Others live to play sports. Still others live to be with their friends. There are other people who like to eat, play sports, *and* be with their friends. But more than anything they like to serve. It is what they live for. These people are the ones who have found the key to happiness.

We could say that the main plan of this book is to help you understand one of God's main plans: Living To Serve.

THE FIRST STEP

Read these popular statements about being a servant. Do you agree or disagree with them? Be prepared to express your opinion about each one to the class.

Statement #1: Caring about others more than yourself is old-fashioned.

Statement #2: If you don't look out for Number One, who will?

Statement #3: If you serve people, they will expect you to be their slave.

Statement #4: If I serve others all of the time, there won't be any time left for myself!

3

Esther, Mordecai, King Xerxes, Haman, and Vashti in one of history's most daring dramas.

ESTHER

This book features the exciting Bible story of Esther. It happened about 500 years before Jesus was born, and takes place in the kingdom of Persia at a time when the Jews were living away from Canaan.

The people you will meet in the story are:

Esther

Esther had grown to be a beautiful young woman. Her parents had died when she was a child, so her cousin, Mordecai, adopted her. As a child playing near the palace, Esther might have dreamed of being the queen, but she could never have guessed that a nation of people would rely on her to save them from an evil massacre.

Mordecai

An officer in the king's household, Mordecai was a faithful Jew and a loyal servant of King Xerxes. He proved his loyalty to the king by uncovering a plot to assassinate him. This brave action later led the king to reward Mordecai in a way that made Haman sorry he ever opened his mouth.

King Xerxes

After King Darius died, Asahuerus, or Xerxes, became king of Persia. King Xerxes seemed to enjoy being a king, and he especially relished the feasts and parties. He was proud of his kingdom and liked showing it off. King Xerxes seemed to trust almost anyone in his palace, which nearly cost him his life and the life of his queen.

Queen Vashti

King Xerxes' pride over his kingdom included his beautiful wife, Vashti. She was not only beautiful, but was stubborn in her ideas about herself. This would one day turn the kingdom – and her crown – upside down.

Haman

Haman loved collecting power for himself. Pride oozed from his words and splashed across his conceited smile. He was able to lie in ways that caused the king and others to believe him. Haman's wickedness kept the Jews hanging in fear, but a sudden turn of events kept Haman hanging forever.

The Henry Project

Tony ran screaming into his house. "Miss Pam! Miss Pam! Call the ambulance. A kid's been hit by a car!"

Miss Pam hurried to the phone, dropping a pile of laundry on the way. Tony ran back outside to join the crowd that had gathered around the boy.

Tony's heart skipped a beat when he realized that the boy was Henry Klinkdale. Henry and Tony, or "Bounce," as his teammates called him, played basketball on the same Boys' Club team. "Henry, it's me, Tony Erving. You know, 'Bounce' . . . from the team." Henry looked toward the familiar voice. "An ambulance is on its way. You're going to be fine. Really!"

"Jerome. Where's Jerome?" whispered Henry.

Tony didn't need to look far to see the scraggly tail of the mutt Henry called Jerome. He was being held back by a well-meaning observer and was only about two feet from Henry's head. "He's right over there," said Tony. "I'll see you at the hospital," yelled Tony as they closed the doors of the van.

Tony's thoughts carried him back three years to the accident that had killed his mother. She had been on her way to buy decorations for his eighth birthday party. Seeing Henry hurt caused Tony to feel ill.

"Tony! Is he going to be all right?" called Miss Pam from the porch. Miss Pam was the Erving's housekeeper. "Yes," hollered Tony. "It looks like

a broken leg. He's a kid who plays on my Boys' Club team and I promised him I would take his dog home. I'll be right back. Okay?"

As Tony and Jerome rounded the corner, Betty Canterbury caught up with them. "I heard about Henry! His dad is our gardener." The closer they got to Henry's house, the poorer looking the houses became. Henry's home was too small for the six children and two parents who lived there, but it was neatly kept. "I like the color they have painted their house," said Betty.

Betty's own house was at least ten times larger than the Klinkdale's home, but she was not one to be snobbish about her wealth. The family was hurrying to their beat up station wagon to go to the hospital, but they stopped long enough to give Tony a sincere thanks for returning Jerome.

The next day at the lunch table, Tony and Betty continued talking about Henry. Their visit to Henry's house had caused them to want to do something to help. "My dad said that Henry has an afternoon paper route that helps pay for his brother's diabetes medicine," said Betty.

Soon David Peterson and Darcie Carlisle had joined them. Darcie didn't know Henry, but David did. He had tutored Henry in reading last quarter. The four began pooling ideas about ways to help Henry. They gradually agreed to a plan of action. David scribbled their ideas onto Tony's lunch sack, then later he transferred them to his computer. The following day, he gave each member of the group a print-out of The Henry Project.

The group had agreed to raise money for another bike for Henry. Betty would make some of her famous seasoned oyster crackers to sell for $1.25 a quart to teachers and neighbors. David would make designer print-outs on his computer for 75¢ each, and Tony would sell one of his four basketballs signed by his dad's cousin, who was a pro basketball player. Darcie would lead the little children on her block in exercises for 25¢ per person.

In addition to raising money for the bike, David agreed to help Henry with his homework until he was able to return to school. Tony and Darcie and Betty would take turns delivering papers every afternoon.

Twenty-three days went by before Henry was released from the hospital wearing a cast and sitting in a wheelchair. Twenty-three days of throwing papers on lawns, raising money, and helping with homework. Twenty-three days of getting to know Henry and his family better. Twenty-three days of being extra tired, extra helpful, and extra happy.

On the day Henry came home, a freshly-painted bike was waiting for him on the lawn. The group had bought it at a garage sale and had worked hard to make it look almost new. Balloons were tied to tree branches, and crepe paper streamers were taped to a "Welcome Home" banner. Betty baked some treats, and Darcie brought a set of colored pens to use in writing on Henry's new cast.

The Henry Project was such a success that the group agreed to look for another project. "This time I want to be on the giving end of it," said Henry. He had become a good friend.

"I can hardly wait to start something new," said Darcie. "This was fun!" Done well, serving others *does* have a way of becoming a happy habit.

INTER**MISSION**

Select one of the following things to do on a separate sheet of paper:
a. Draw a picture of Henry's yard on the day he came home from the hospital.
b. Write out a page which you think resembles David's print-out sheet.
c. Write a thank-you note to the group as if it were from Henry.

UNIT ONE
Serving by Sharing

"Share with God's people who are in need." Romans 12:13

WISDOM ◆ **OBEDIENCE** ◆ **PUNCTUALITY**

WISDOM

Serving by Sharing Wisdom

Bible words:
"Listen to advice and accept instruction, and in the end you will be wise." Proverbs 19:20

LESSON LEARNING

Jeffrey slammed his desk top down. "Man, I wish this day was over. I'm sick of school already," he said. "In fact, I can hardly wait for the day when I can stop this learning stuff." David Peterson was seated next to Jeffrey and said, "Don't be ridiculous! Learning lasts your whole life!"

Jeffrey grunted and said, "Not **my** whole life. I know all I need to know," he said.

"By saying that, you're proving that you **don't** know all you need to know." David had a way of saying things as they really were.

David was from a family of learners. His father was Dr. William Peterson, a professor at the university. His mother, Diane, was a computer analyst. They knew many things, but they enjoyed learning more. In fact, David's father was still taking classes.

The Petersons, including David's fourth grade brother, didn't just know about facts, however. They also liked to learn about life, and they were each willing to take advice.

1. What is the meaning of "advice"? _____

_____

2. What advice have you received from your mother or father recently? _____

_____

3. What advice have you received from your teacher this week? Your friends? Be ready to share your answers with the class. _____

_____

4. Why does accepting advice and instruction make a person look smart rather than stupid? _____

_____

5. Does anyone, except God, know everything?   **Yes** _____ **No** _____

   Do you expect anyone to know everything?   **Yes** _____ **No** _____

   Does anyone expect you to know everything?   **Yes** _____ **No** _____

6. There is good advice and bad advice. What would be good advice for a person who is lost? _____

_____

   What would bad advice be for the same person? _____

_____

_____

7. What people in your life give you good advice? _____

_____

8. What advice would you give Jeffrey? _____

_____

   Do you think he would follow your advice?   **Yes** _____ **No** _____

KNOW-IT-ALLS and LEARN-IT-ALLS

Know-it-alls like to pretend they do, which is silly because everyone knows they don't! Learn-it-alls like to admit they don't know it all, which is great because they don't.

What would a Know-It-All and Learn-It-All do in these situations?

SITUATIONS	KNOW-IT-ALL	LEARN-IT-ALL
1. A guest visits class to talk about reptiles.		
2. A boy in class gets a new computer.		
3. The teacher divides the class into groups to report on life in Latin America.		
4. A girl in class is going to Hawaii.		

GOD'S ADVICE

Copy the Bible words about wisdom from page 9 onto these lines: _____
_____
_____

Do you think this is good advice?   **Yes** _____   **No** _____

How would you serve a Know-It-All by sharing advice? _____
_____
_____

Definition:
Doing what I am told to do.

◆ **OBEDIENCE** ◆

Serving by Doing What I'm Told

Opposite:
Doing what I am told not to do.

Bible words:
"A mocker resents correction; he will not consult the wise." Proverbs 15:12

Sharing The Load

The day Henry said, "I wish we could think of a way to let the teachers know we appreciate them" was the day the group's second project began.

Because of his cast, Henry had been helping Mrs. Maddux in the art room instead of going to PE. He was amazed at how much work she had to do every day. At lunch, he would talk about it to the group.

"I hardly ever see a teacher leave the school without carrying work home," said Betty. The others agreed.

And so, when Henry spoke his wish about showing appreciation, all the members of the group were ready to do something about it. What they did was plan a Be-Good-to-Teacher Week.

As usual, David was quick to make things official with a computer print-out of their Agreement to Appreciate. It contained the plans of the Be-Good-to-Teacher project. They wanted to obey and help in such a way that teachers would have no doubt about their appreciation. Beyond that, they would wow them with small and big surprises.

The project was to begin officially the following Monday. On the Friday before, Tony bounced his basketball into the classroom and rolled it under his desk. Basketball season was about to begin, and he wanted to use every extra minute to get ready.

"Tony, the basketball belongs in your locker or the gym, not in class," said Mr. Newman. "For today, bring it here and I'll keep it for you."

"What?! It's not hurting anything here, Mr. Newman. Please, can I keep it with me?"

"No. You can't," answered the teacher. The other students in the class were listening carefully, waiting to see what Tony would do. They knew how he felt about his basketball.

Tony stayed in his seat, pretending to stare at his pencil. Mr. Newman remained in the front of the room, waiting for Tony to obey. No one made a sound. It was David who broke the silence. "Come on, Tony. Just give it to him."

"Why should I? It's my basketball," answered Tony. It was not like him to disobey, but he did have a temper that sometimes got him into trouble.

"Because he is the teacher and you are the student," said David. "He's not being unreasonable, Tony. You are." David never was afraid to say what he thought.

Tony got up slowly, to everyone's relief, and handed Mr. Newman the basketball. As he did, he said, "Mr. Conroy let me keep it with me last year."

By lunchtime, everyone in the group had heard about Tony's display of disobedience. "This is just great," said David. "Three days before we begin the Be-Good-to-Teacher Week, someone decides to be **bad** to a teacher."

"Knock it off, David," said Tony. "How was I supposed to know that he didn't understand basketball like Mr. Conroy does?" He paused. "Besides, I still say I'm right and I'm going to do it again tomorrow."

Betty let out a big sigh, and Darcie rolled her eyes in disbelief. "I think we should postpone our project until this gets worked out," said Betty. The others agreed, except Tony. He stomped off to the court, his beloved basketball under his arm.

That afternoon, when Tony was delivering papers, he was surprised to see Mr. Newman outside playing basketball with a man on Henry's paper route. "Hi, Tony," he shouted. "Want to shoot some hoops?"

"No, thanks. I have to finish delivering papers," said Tony.

"Okay. But you're welcome to join us on your way back."

Tony had never refused to play basketball in his life. He thought about it during the route. Along the way, he met David. "Hi, David."

"Hi, Tony," he said. "How are you feeling about things by now?"

"You won't believe who I just saw playing basketball," said Tony.

"Yes, I would. I just saw him down the street," said David. "Mr. Newman is a nice man, Tony. He just doesn't want basketballs being bounced and stored in his room."

"But what does it hurt?" asked Tony.

"Tony, does your basketball help you think about math?" asked David. "And if you were a teacher, would you want a basketball in your room?"

Tony didn't really want to answer David's honest questions. "You're hiding from the truth, Tony. Better to admit it now than later when Mr. Newman has to call your dad about your disobedience."

"Well, we'll see," said Tony, throwing the last of his papers.

On his way back, Tony could see Mr. Newman sitting on the curb waiting for him. "Hi, Tony. Ready to play?"

"I guess," said Tony. He could tell Mr. Newman was glad. Tony always did like Mr. Newman's smile. They played until both of them had won at least two games. By the time they were through, Tony was feeling a little foolish. "Why did I have to make such a scene today," he wondered.

"About today, Tony," Mr. Newman said as he wiped his face with his shirt.

"Never mind," said Tony. "I acted like a fool. It's just that I love basketball so much."

"So do I," said Mr. Newman. "But loving basketball is not the issue. Obedience is the issue."

"I know. I guess I don't have to have my basketball with me in class. I'm sorry I did what I did, Mr. Newman," said Tony.

"I forgive you, Tony," said Mr. Newman. "I'd like to stay, but I have to go inside and correct some papers before dinner."

"Do you need some help?" asked Tony. He didn't think anyone would mind if Be-Good-to-Teacher Week started a few days early.

inter**MISSION**

Which person in the story are you most like? _____

In what way are you like this person? _____

_____

Definition:
Being on time.

PUNCTUALITY

Opposite:
Being late.

Serving by Being on Time

Bible words:
"As vinegar to the teeth and smoke to the eyes, so is a sluggard to those who send him." Proverbs 10:26

PUNCTUALITY PAYS

1. Would you choose to stand in a trail of smoke with your eyes open? Why? _____
   _____

2. Is vinegar one of your favorite drinks?   **Yes** _____   **No** _____

3. What is the meaning of "sluggard"? _____
   _____

4. Read the verse about punctuality. God is saying that sending a sluggard on an errand is as pleasant as
   _____
   _____

5. What word would you say describes the person who is the opposite of a sluggard? _____
   _____

6. Use the word from #5 to write out your version of a proverb that describes the joy of sending such
   a person on an errand.
   "As _____ , so is a _____
   to those who send him."

7. It could be said that PUNCTUALITY PAYS. Be ready to talk about the rewards of being punctual. Also,
   think about unhappy moments the punctual person misses.

PROMPT AND NOT-SO-PROMPT

Darcie moaned loudly when Mr. Black asked the class to turn in their book reports. Hers was undone and at home under a stack of snapshots of last summer's vacation. What do you think Darcie might have been doing instead of writing her book report? _____ _____ _____

Tony spun around the corner just as the class was saying "with liberty and justice for all." "At least I made it before they finished the flag salute," he thought. What do you think was the reason for Tony's frequent tardiness? _____ _____ _____

Betty, David, and **Henry** also had areas of their lives that were prompt and not-so-prompt. We all do unless we learn punctuality. On this chart, design a schedule that you believe is reasonable for a sixth grader to follow. Include time for each of the activities listed below the chart.

PUNCTUALITY PLAN

ACTIVITY	TIME
Before School: _____	_____
_____	_____
_____	_____
_____	_____
_____	_____
After School: _____	_____
_____	_____
_____	_____
_____	_____
_____	_____
_____	_____
_____	_____
_____	_____
_____	_____
_____	_____

ACTIVITIES:
Time with God   Homework   Preparing for school   Relaxation
Chores   Mealtime   Room straightened

PUNCTUALITY PUZZLER: In what New Testament story was Jesus accused of being late?

King Xerxes is furious over Vashti's disobedience.

ESTHER

BACK FIRE

King Xerxes had been showing off his wealth and majesty to the leaders of the land for 180 days, and now he wanted to end it with a week-long banquet.

He chose to hold the splendid affair in the enclosed garden. Lovely blue and white banners hung from silver rings attached to marble pillars. Gold and silver couches were arranged in a festive way on a floor of costly stones, and each guest was served the wine of his choice in a gold goblet with its own design. The king loved to be generous, and it showed.

After seven days of eating and drinking, King Xerxes' drunk mind came up with an idea. "Servants, tell Vashti to prepare herself! I want to display her beauty to my guests!"

At the same time the king was giving his banquet, Queen Vashti was giving a party for the women of the palace. When the servants brought her the message from the king, she stubbornly refused. "I will not do this!" she said. Vashti knew what kinds of wrong things women were asked to do in front of drunken men at banquets. The women were shocked! It was not an everyday thing to disobey an order from the king.

The servants carried her message back to King Xerxes. When he heard it, he burned with anger. He felt embarrassed in front of his friends because his wife had refused to obey him. "I must do something to show everyone that she cannot get away with this," he thought, with muddled mind.

He needed advice from experts of the law to tell him what he could do to Vashti. "What shall I do to Vashti for disobeying my command?" he asked.

The men were close friends of the king and shared his horror at what had happened. One friend spoke up and said, "Vashti not only did wrong against you, she did wrong against all of us. When our wives find out that the queen disobeyed you, they will disobey us. They will say, 'If Vashti does it, so can I!' He added, "There will be no end to the disrespect and discord in our homes!"

All of the men agreed, and their worried whispers floated in and out around the blasts of fury from the king. "What you should do," said Memucan, "is issue a decree that can never be changed. It should say that Vashti can never again enter the presence of the king and that she will be replaced as your queen. By doing this, all of the women of the kingdom will be forced to respect their husbands!"

The men and the king agreed that this was an excellent idea. King Xerxes ordered the decree to be written in the language of every province. It was delivered immediately and proclaimed that every man was to be ruler over his own household.

No decree, however, could remove the memory of the day the queen refused the king's command and put a sour ending on his party.

BACK TO BACK FIRE

BACKFIRE 1

1. What were some of the things that King Xerxes did to make his week-long banquet special?

_____

_____

2. What idea did he come up with after seven days of eating and drinking?

_____

_____

3. How did Vashti respond to the king's request?

_____

_____

4. What emotions do you think Vashti felt as she considered her response to the king?

_____

_____

5. Do you believe that Vashti was right in disobeying the king?

_____

_____

6. Put yourself in King Xerxes' place. What would **you** have done to Vashti in this situation?

_____

_____

7. Pretend you are listening to the king's advisors discussing their own fears. What are some of the things you might hear?

_____

_____

8. Identify any parts of the story that show wisdom or foolishness.

_____

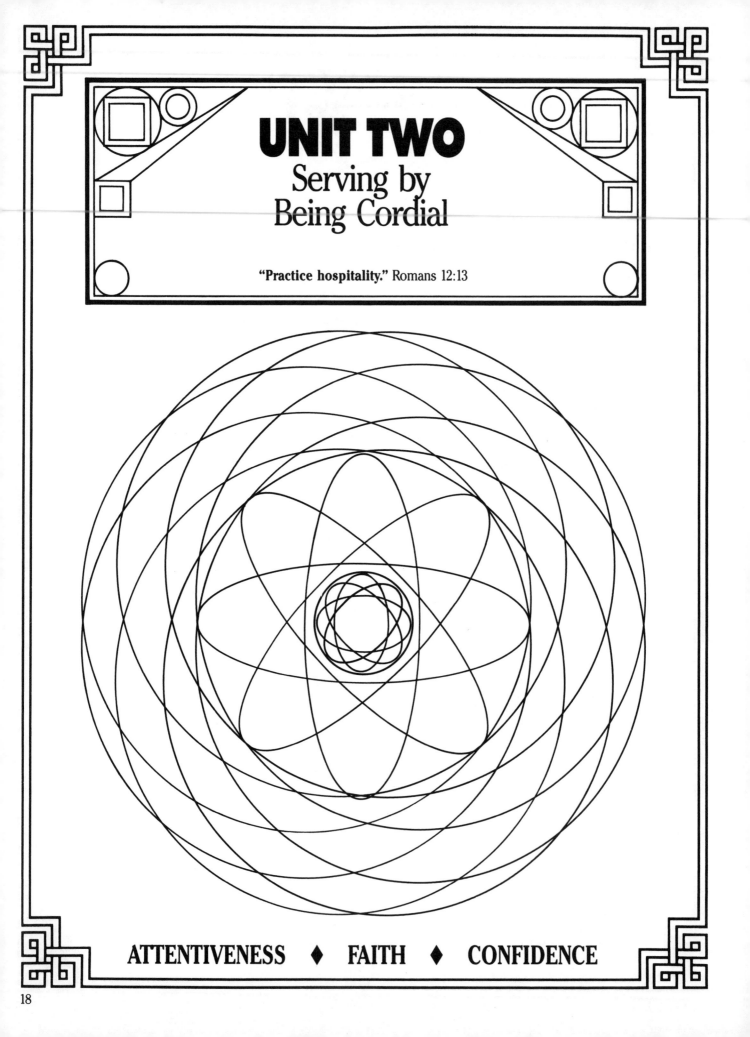

UNIT TWO
Serving by Being Cordial

"Practice hospitality." Romans 12:13

ATTENTIVENESS ♦ **FAITH** ♦ **CONFIDENCE**

ATTENTIVENESS

Serving by Paying Attention

Bible words:

"Why do you look at the speck of sawdust in your brother's eye and pay no attention to the plank in your own eye? How can you say to your brother, 'Brother, let me take the speck out of your eye,' when you yourself fail to see the plank in your own eye? You hypocrite, first take the plank out of your eye, and then you will see clearly to remove the speck from your brother's eye." Luke 6:41-42

BLOCKED VISION

On his way to shoot hoops in the gym, Peter tried to pick three fights. Once inside the gym, he called a fifth grader a name and headed toward Tony, who was practicing his free throws. He had made seven shots in a row and was beginning his eighth when Peter stepped up behind Tony, stomping his foot loudly and yelling "Miss it!" The ball missed the hoop, and Tony whirled around angrily. "Peter, knock it off!"

"Oh, Tony, it was only a little joke. You have such a temper-problem," said Peter. He picked up the ball and began shooting lay-ups while Tony got control of himself.

What was Peter's problem, or fault? _____

What was Tony's problem, or fault? _____

Peter had a common problem: He saw the fault of others but was blind to his own. Jesus thinks this problem is very ugly. In fact, while He was on earth Jesus was trailed and heckled by a group of men called Pharisees who were experts at paying attention to the wrongs of others and ignoring their own. They were leaders who made rules that no one could keep. Even they could not keep them, but they pretended that they could.

Jesus spoke out against their unfairness and pride and they hated Him for it.

THE PHARISEES

To find out more about the Pharisees, look up these verses. You will see the kinds of things the Pharisees said and did. You will also read some of the very words Jesus spoke to them.

In the space next to the verses, write the facts of what was said or done.

VERSES	WHAT WAS SAID OR DONE
Matthew 12:1-13	_____
Matthew 23:1-7	_____
Matthew 23:23, 24	_____
Matthew 23:25, 26	_____
Matthew 23:27, 28	_____
Mark 7:1-8	_____
Luke 18:10-14	_____

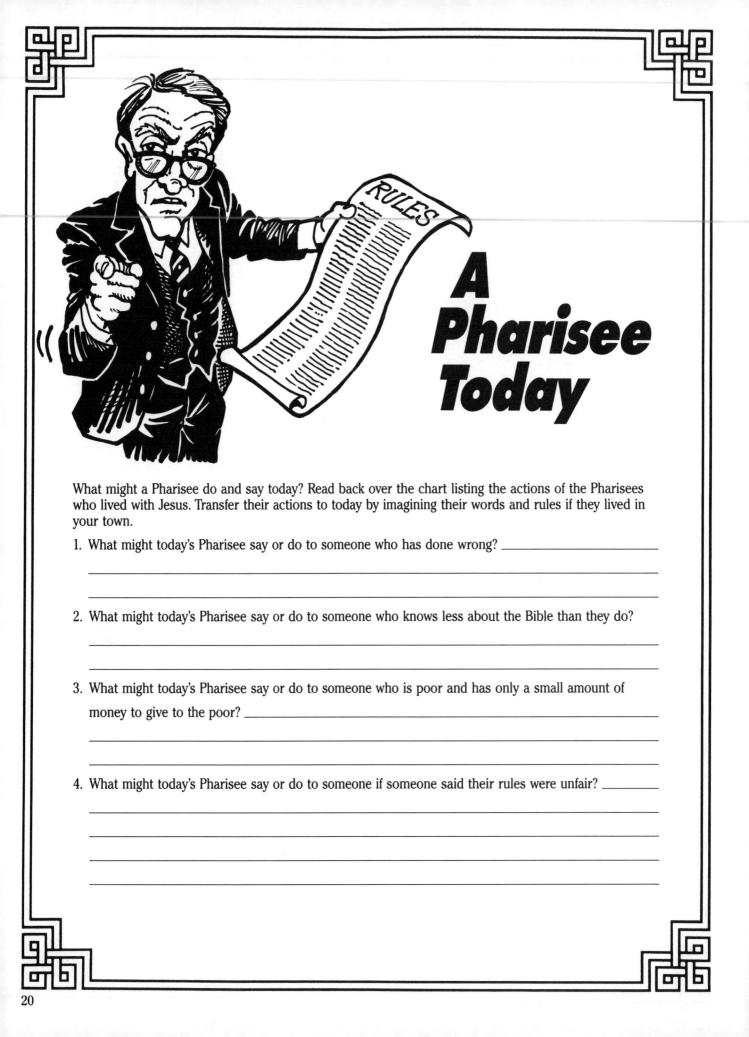

A Pharisee Today

What might a Pharisee do and say today? Read back over the chart listing the actions of the Pharisees who lived with Jesus. Transfer their actions to today by imagining their words and rules if they lived in your town.

1. What might today's Pharisee say or do to someone who has done wrong? _____
   _____
   _____

2. What might today's Pharisee say or do to someone who knows less about the Bible than they do?
   _____
   _____

3. What might today's Pharisee say or do to someone who is poor and has only a small amount of
   money to give to the poor? _____
   _____
   _____

4. What might today's Pharisee say or do to someone if someone said their rules were unfair? _____
   _____
   _____
   _____
   _____

A search for the new queen begins.

ESTHER

When the king got over the shock of Vashti's refusal to display herself in front of his friends, it was suggested that he search for a new queen. "Let's put a person in every province of the kingdom," said a friend of the king. "He will look over all of the young women in his section of the land and bring the most beautiful to the palace. The young woman that pleases you the most will replace Vashti as queen." The king liked the idea and ordered the search to begin.

In the city of Susa, the chairman of the beauty search gathered all of the young women together. Among them was Esther, a Jewish girl who was lovely in every way. Esther was her Persian name. Her real name was Hadassah.

Esther's parents had died when she was young. She grew up under the care of her cousin Mordecai, a fine man who worked as an officer in the household of King Xerxes.

Esther was chosen to return to the palace as one of the candidates for the queen contest. Hegai was the leader of the team who would prepare the girls for their visit with the king.

He thought that Esther was more lovely than the rest, and he quickly began taking special care of her. He ordered her maids to give her beauty treatments and special food, and gave Esther the best place to stay.

Mordecai must have missed having Esther at home with him. He walked past the courtyard every day hoping to catch a glimpse of her or

perhaps speak a few words. She often sent messages to him with one of her maids.

All of the girls in the queen contest had to complete twelve months of beauty treatments. For the first six months they were treated with oil and myrrh, and for the second six months they were treated with perfumes and cosmetics. Each girl would have a turn with the king. The girl who pleased him the most would be the new queen.

When it was Esther's turn, Hegai gave her advice about what to wear. She followed his advice, and everyone who saw her thought she was the loveliest girl of all. The king agreed and pronounced Esther queen instead of Vashti.

King Xerxes set a royal crown on Esther's head and then gave a great banquet in her honor. He gave everyone a holiday and gave them gifts.

One of the first things Esther did as queen was tell the king about two men who had plotted to kill him. Mordecai was the one who discovered their plans, and his loyal act was written down in the record book of the king.

As a child, Esther had obeyed and loved Mordecai. As queen, she wisely continued in her love and obedience toward him. She must have felt very proud of his bravery, and he must have been equally pleased with her success as queen.

BACKFIRE 2

1. How was King Xerxes going to select a new queen?

_____

_____

2. What were some of the details of Esther's life presented in this story?

_____

_____

3. Who was the leader of the queen-to-be preparation team and what did he do to prepare the girls for the contest?

_____

_____

4. How was Esther's attentiveness important to her being chosen by the king?

_____

_____

5. What was one of the first things Esther did as queen? What does this tell you about Esther's character?

_____

_____

6. How did Esther display obedience in this story?

_____

_____

7. Put yourself in the place of King Xerxes. What qualities would **you** have looked for in a girl trying to be your queen?

_____

_____

Definition:
Believing God will do
what He says He will
do.

FAITH

Serving by Believing God

Bible words:

"And what more shall I say? I do not have time to tell about Gideon, Barak, Samson, Jephthah, David, Samuel, and the prophets, who through faith conquered kingdoms, administered justice, and gained what was promised; who shut the mouths of lions, quenched the fury of the flames, and escaped the edge of the sword; whose weakness was turned to strength; and who became powerful in battle and routed foreign armies." Hebrews 11:32-34

FAITH IS THE 🔑 TO GOD'S POWER!

SOMETHING IN COMMON

The people who are mentioned in Hebrews 11:32-34 had something in common: Faith! They had something else in common as well. Write words 56, 57, 58, 59 and 60 from Hebrews 11:32 on these lines to discover what else the faith heroes shared:

_____ _____ _____ _____ _____ .
        56   57   58   59   60

PAUL'S PROBLEM

1. The Apostle Paul had a problem that made him weak. He asked Jesus to remove the problem three times, but Jesus said:

   " _____

   _____

   _____

   _____ "

   Sometimes, then, Jesus chooses to let our problems remain so that His power can explode in us as it did in the list of people in Hebrews 11.

HEBREWS HEROES

2. How did God's power explode in the lives of the Hebrews heroes? Look up their exciting stories in these verses, then explain how God showed His power.

   a. Gideon, Judges 6:11-16 _____

   b. Barak, Judges 4:4-22 _____

   c. Samson, Judges 16:17-30 _____

   d. Jephthah, Judges 11:1-10, 32, 33 _____

   e. David, I Sam. 17:33, 38-51 _____

   f. Samuel, I Sam. 3:10-20 _____

Faith is out of Sight!

God loves faith! In fact, He says that it is impossible to please Him without faith! (Read it for yourself in Hebrews 11:6.) When we put our faith, or trust, in God, we are telling Him that we believe He will take care of us in the best way.

TRUST GOD

Match these examples of faith.

1. David shows faith when he studies for a test, then . . .

2. Henry shows faith when he promises to try to earn money, then . . .

3. Darcie shows faith when she asks God to help her be friendly, then . . .

4. Tony shows faith by admitting to God that he has let his anger get out of control, then . . .

5. Betty shows faith when she is afraid at night, then . . .

. . . trusts God to help him find a part-time job.

. . . trusts God to forgive him.

. . . trusts God to keep her safe.

. . . trusts God to remind him of the correct answer.

. . . trusts Him to give her people to befriend.

How has someone you know shown faith?

Bible words:

"So we say with confidence, 'The Lord is my helper; I will not be afraid. What can man do to me?' Remember your leaders, who spoke the word of God to you. Consider the outcome of their way of life and imitate their faith. Jesus Christ is the same yesterday and today and forever." Hebrews 13:6-8

It's Over!

The same nightmare woke Henry up three times in one night. In it, the doctor would remove his cast and everyone would cheer. They would then beg Henry to walk without his crutches. But when he would step down on his leg, it would break again.

The nightmares frightened Henry. It made him wish that the doctor was not removing his cast right after breakfast that morning. "What if my nightmare comes true?"

Other fears joined the first. "What if it hurts a lot?" "What if I have a limp?" "What if my broken leg looks different than the other one?" By the time Henry arrived at the doctor's office, he had a large collection of fears waiting to rob him of the happiness at having the itchy cast removed.

Dr. Simmons worked quickly and gently. At any minute, Henry would see his leg for the first time in six weeks. "I hope I recognize it," he thought. At first, Henry would only peek at his leg. "It looks familiar," he thought. "Maybe a little pale, but it matches my other one." Relief chased one of his fears away, but the others hung around to bother him.

Dr. Simmons gave Henry instructions and a list of exercises to do every day. "Use the crutches until you feel confident about walking again."

"He'll be walking in no time," said Mr. Klinkdale. He had taken the morning off so that he could be with Henry at the doctor's office. "I know he will," said Dr. Simmons.

Henry was embarrassed by his silly fears. If he had talked about them to someone, he would have found out that his fears were normal. Instead, Henry decided he wouldn't tell anyone about them except God. Henry had trusted Him for other things, so he knew God would help him with this, too.

"Hey, Henry, your leg looks good." Tony had caught up with him in the hall. "The people on your paper route are going to be happy to see you back soon."

Henry didn't know what to say, so he just smiled. He missed the people on his paper route, too, but pedaling a bike might hurt a leg that has been broken.

"Well, look at you, Henry Klinkdale," said Mrs. Maddux. "It looks like you'll be back in PE soon. I'm glad for you, but I will surely miss your help." Henry and Mrs. Maddux had become good friends.

"Henry!" yelled Betty and Darcie. "Wait up for us." They had just gotten off their bus. "Let us see your leg."

"Oh, I miss seeing my signature on your cast. Do you mind if I write on your leg?" Darcie asked with a giggle.

Henry walked with them to class. He believed that he had kept his fears from showing in front of his friends, but he was wrong. All of them noticed.

"I think something is wrong with Henry," said Betty. She had a warm heart toward people in need.

The others agreed. "I think he's afraid to walk on his leg. That's what happened to my neighbor when she broke her leg."

"Well, then, we'd better do what we can to help him," said David, getting out his pencil.

"We don't need a print-out on this one, David," said Betty. "We just need common sense." Each of them chose one thing to do for Henry.

That afternoon Tony walked home with Henry. "You know, when my neighbor broke her leg, she was afraid to walk on it. She was afraid it would break again. Her doctor said that's a normal feeling."

"Really?" said Henry. "That's interesting." Inside himself, Henry was much more interested than he was letting on and Tony knew it.

Two days later, Betty gave an oral report on broken bones and how strong they heal. Henry paid more attention to her report than any of the others that were given that day.

David dropped by Henry's house and asked him if he would show him the exercises he did every day. Henry hadn't done them for two days, so David's visit made Henry's mother very happy. "Come back anytime," she said as David left. The next day and every other day for a week he helped Henry with his exercises.

"Henry! The field trip to the science center is in one week," said Darcie. "It's too bad you'll have to go with your crutches. Oh well, you'll still have fun."

The group checked up on Henry's progress often. "It's going to be so great to see him without those pesky crutches," said Darcie. "Yes, but **when,**" said David.

The night before the field trip, Henry decided to try to walk normally around his room. His old fears tried to keep him from it, but Henry chose not to pay attention to them. With a deep breath, Henry got up and pretended that both legs were strong. By the time he got to the door, he realized that he wasn't pretending. Both legs **were** strong!

The phone rang and, without thinking, Henry ran to answer it. His family stopped what they were doing to stare at Henry. Their wide eyes made Henry laugh. "It's for you, Mom," said Henry. She came to the phone wiping her wet cheeks. The last time Henry had seen her cry was the day he had been hit by the car. That was all behind him now.

That night Henry kept waking up, but not because of nightmares. Henry's mind was feeding him pictures of his happy friends. He imagined seeing their faces when he hopped off the bus without his crutches. God had helped Henry walk by putting people around him to give him confidence.

When Henry finally fell asleep, it was with a grin on his lips and a hand on his strong leg.

INTER**MISSION**

In what other ways could Henry have handled his fears?

UNIT THREE
Serving by Being
Kind to Our Enemies

"Bless those who persecute you; bless and do not curse." Romans 12:14

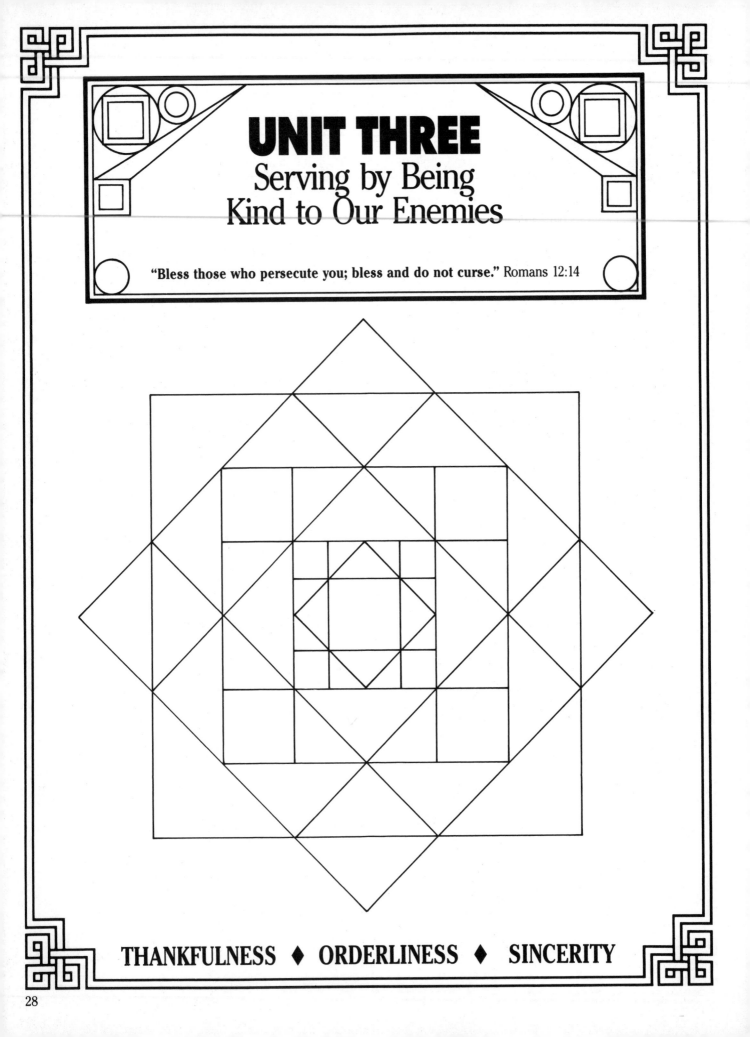

THANKFULNESS ◆ ORDERLINESS ◆ SINCERITY

Mordecai refuses to bow to Haman.

ESTHER

EPISODE THREE

BACK FIRE

It took a good long time for the excitement over Queen Esther to subside. When it did, King Xerxes made another announcement that quickly spread through the kingdom.

The announcement said, "Let it be known that Haman, son of Hammedatha, the Agagite, has been promoted to a seat of honor higher than all other leaders. Everyone will bow in honor to him."

Haman loved being important. He bragged about himself to his family and friends and liked giving orders at the palace. When he would walk through the palace gates, the people there would bow to him. He especially loved this part of his job. It gave him even more reason to strut about in a conceited way.

When Haman walked through the gate past Mordecai, however, Mordecai would not bow. At first, Haman did not notice. The guards at the gate tried to convince Mordecai to give honor to Haman, but Mordecai refused. They told Haman that Mordecai was not bowing to him. Haman did not like the news.

The next time Haman passed through the gate, he looked for Mordecai. It was easy to find him, because he was the only one standing. Each time this happened, Haman became more angry and the wickedness of his plan against Mordecai grew more evil.

Haman had found out that Mordecai was a Jew. "I won't kill just Mordecai," thought Haman. "I'll trick the king into killing all of the Jews in Persia! Yes! That's what I'll do."

The first step of the evil trick was choosing a day for the slaughter to take place. It would happen on the thirteenth day of the month of Adar. The next step would be getting permission from the king to carry out the plan. Haman was an expert liar, and his practice of stretching the truth served him as he spoke to the king.

"King Xerxes, there is a certain group of people scattered around your kingdom who keep themselves separate from the rest of us. They have different customs, and they do not obey your laws. It isn't in your best interest to tolerate this." Then Haman added, "I will be glad to add about 10,000 talents of silver to your treasury to help pay the soldiers to destroy these people."

"Keep the money," said the king, "and do with them as you please." King Xerxes removed his ring and gave it to Haman. This meant that he was giving Haman permission to do anything he wanted.

Haman called the palace secretaries together and wrote out the decree in everyone's language. Haman sealed each copy of the degree with the imprint of the king's own ring. This showed that the king approved of the plan. The notice said that on the thirteenth of Adar all Jewish men, women, and children would be killed.

Haman was pleased with himself. The king had fallen for his trick, and soon Mordecai and everyone like him would pay for their mistake. What Haman did not know was that Esther was also a Jew.

BACK TO BACKFIRE

(logo: BACK TO BACK FIRE)

BACKFIRE 3

1. What announcement did King Xerxes make after the excitement about Queen Esther died down?

_____

_____

2. What was the one part of his job that Haman loved best?

_____

_____

3. Who was the only person who would not bow to Haman and why was it so easy to pick him out of the crowd at the gate?

_____

_____

4. Do you believe Haman overreacted to Mordecai's behavior? What would you have done in Haman's place?

_____

_____

5. Was the king wise in giving his seal of approval to Haman's plan? Should he have been more attentive to why Haman wanted to do this?

_____

_____

6. Describe the details of Haman's orderly plan for revenge against Mordecai.

_____

_____

7. What did Haman sincerely want in this story?

_____

_____

THANKFULNESS

Definition:
Being glad for the goodness of God and others.

Opposite:
Being blind to the goodness of God and others.

Serving by Being Grateful

Bible words:
"Come, let us sing for joy to the Lord; let us shout aloud to the Rock of our salvation. Let us come before Him with thanksgiving and extol Him with music and song. For the Lord is the great God, the great King above all gods." Psalm 95:1-3

DAVID AND THANKFULNESS

David's father bought a program for his computer that contained the entire Bible. Because David had been careful with the other programs he had borrowed, his father let him use the Bible program.

One day, after studying thankfulness in school, David decided to ask the computer to show him the verses in the Bible with "thanks" in them. How many verses do you think the computer showed him?

_____ verses.

Use your computer mind to locate a verse in the book of Psalms with a form of "thank" in it. Select one you think says "thank you" in a way you would like to say it to God.

My Thanks Choice: _____

_____

_____

David thought about something his mother had said to him last week. "David, I hardly ever hear a thankful word come out of your mouth," she said.

"I'm thankful inside, Mom," said David. "I just don't say it much."

David is good at giving advice to others. What would you say is good advice for him about expressing thankfulness?

_____

_____

_____

_____

THINK THANKS

Think of five things that God has done that deserve your thanks. Write them on a separate sheet of paper. As you write each item, say "thank you" to God for it.

DIRECTOR OF CELEBRATION

Imagine that you have been named Director of Celebration. It is your job to plan an event for your class that shows how thankful you are for God's goodness.

You are asked to follow the ideas in Psalm 95:1-3 for your Thankfulness Celebration. Fill in this plan sheet with your ideas.

My Celebration Plan Sheet

1. A Song of Joy
"Come, let us sing for joy to the Lord."

My choice for a song of joy:

_____

2. A Shout
"Let us shout aloud to the rock of our salvation."

My choice for words to shout:

_____

_____

3. A Word of Thanks
"Let us come before Him with thanksgiving."

My choice for words of thanks:

_____

_____

_____

4. A Song of Praise
"Let us extol Him with music and song."

My choice for a song of praise:

_____

5. A Grand Finale
"For the Lord is the great God, the great King above all gods."

My choice for a grand finale:

_____

_____

_____

_____

_____

Definition:
Putting plans and things
in their right place.

ORDERLINESS

Serving by Being Organized

Opposite:
Allowing things and
plans to become
confusing.

Bible words:
"Then Esther sent this reply to Mordecai: 'Go, gather together all the Jews who are in Susa, and fast for me. Do not eat or drink for three days, night or day. I and my maids will fast as you do. When this is done, I will go to the king, even though it is against the law. And if I perish, I perish'." Esther 4:15-17

ORDERLY GOD

No one does a finer job of showing orderliness than God. He keeps plans and things in their place. The weather is one example of God's orderliness. The worlds of plants and animals are others, as are music and mathematics.

Give one example of God's orderliness in each of these examples.

God's orderliness in:

WEATHER _____

PLANTS _____

ANIMALS _____

MUSIC _____

MATHEMATICS _____

ORDERLY ESTHER

In the verse for orderliness, Esther is sending a message to Mordecai asking him to organize the Jews into a giant prayer group. Later in the story you will see why she needed their prayers.

For now, think **back** to the facts of the Esther stories you have read so far. Name three of the many signs of orderliness in the story of Esther.

Signs of Orderliness in Esther's Story

Example: King Xerxes sent invitations to government leaders to attend his party.

1. _____

_____

2. _____

_____

3. _____

_____

ORDERLY YOU

As Director of Celebration in the Thankfulness section of this unit, you planned ways to show thankfulness to God. Now you have been named Director of Special Events.

Study the "Job Description and Guidelines" below to learn what you are to do. Complete your project on a separate sheet of paper.

MEMO

TO: DIRECTOR OF SPECIAL EVENTS
FROM: COUNCIL OF ORDERLINESS
SUBJECT: JOB DESCRIPTION AND GUIDELINES

This is to inform you of your responsibilities as Director of Special Events. You are to:

1. Plan a special event of your choice. It must be for the purpose of helping a person or group.

2. Organize each part of the special event.

3. Put others in charge of each part and instruct them about their duties.

4. Plan a budget using no more than $200.00.

5. Write out your plans and budget, the names of your helpers and their jobs, and the dates each part of your plan will be completed.

6. With your plans include a sketch of the poster that will announce your special event.

Thank you for your willingness to serve in this important position.

Definition:
Truly meaning what I
say and do.

SINCERITY

Serving by Being "Real"

Bible words:
"Like clouds and wind without rain is a man who boasts of gifts he does not give." Proverbs 25:14

Opposite:
Pretending that I mean
what I say and do.

Big Promises

Darcie meant well when she promised the pre-schoolers that she would bring a clown and presents and lots of food to them on Thursday. But here it was Monday and she had no clown or presents and no sign of special food.

Darcie's plan had been part of the fourth project for the group. Each member was to do something for young children. The idea had come from a visit David had made to his cousin's hospital room when she was having her tonsils out. David wasn't one to get worked up about things, but when he saw all of the children there, he wanted to help them.

He had returned with a video that he and his father had filmed the summer before in their backyard. It was called "The Mystery of the Buried Footprints." His mother had sent along some popcorn for the kids to eat while they watched the video.

Darcie lived near a pre-school. She received permission to be a helper for two weeks as part of the group's project. One day when she was reading a book to the children about parties, she got carried away and promised them the biggest party they had ever had. Now, one week later, she was sorry about the promise.

The party had become an unpleasant thought to Darcie because she had realized that it was not going to work out. Darcie didn't like thinking unpleasant thoughts, so she chose not to think about the party at all. That only worked for one

day, however, and by Tuesday Darcie was upset and tearful. When she and Betty were alone, Darcie told her the ugly story.

"You have to tell the kids that you can't give them the party you promised," advised Betty.

"No, I can't do that!" cried Darcie. "It'll make them sad."

"Well, then, what are you going to do?" asked Betty.

"I don't know. My dad can't be the clown because he's going out of town. I've spent my allowance on other things so I can't buy the balloons. And Mom says she doesn't have time to make anything more than cookies this week for the kids."

Betty listened and comforted her friend. When Darcie left, she was glad for Betty's kindness, but she didn't feel much better about things. Out loud she said, "I hope I'll think about my words before I make any more big promises."

"Darcie! Darcie! Come here!" The children at the pre-school had spotted her. "Only two days until our party."

"Uh, yes. Two days . . ." mumbled Darcie.

The day of the party arrived too soon to suit her. She dreaded showing up with just a little plate of cookies and one big excuse. Darcie may have gotten carried away with her promises, but she was no coward. She would face the kids and tell them the truth. "We'll have our party," she thought. "But it will just be a simple one." She was worried that the children would hate her for it.

Darcie greeted the pre-schoolers with a half-hearted smile. All of them were waiting for her in an eager circle. "Where are the balloons and clown?" they asked. Darcie stepped closer to them to break the bad news. "Well, about the party. It, uh. Well, sometimes things don't . . . I mean . . ."

While Darcie was struggling with her words, Tony was outside struggling with the clown suit he had secretly borrowed from Darcie's father. He was surprised to see David walking to the door with pink and yellow balloons. "Hey, I didn't know you were going to be here," said Tony.

David looked surprised. "Me neither, as a matter of fact," said David. "Betty called me last night and asked if I would deliver some balloons to this pre-school."

"Same here. It looks as if Betty has a project of her own going here," said Tony.

Betty's voice reached them from the sidewalk. "Go on in. Hurry! We'll be late." She was carrying two boxes of goodies that she and her mother had made the night before.

Tony and David opened the door in time to hear Darcie fumbling for words and finally saying, "There won't be a big party, kids."

"What do you mean, there won't be a big party," said Tony in a clown voice that surprised even him. "**I'm** here, and where **I** am there are **big** parties!"

"Darcie, you were just fooling us!" said Susan, a brown-eyed three-year old. Darcie was too surprised to speak.

Henry managed to finish his paper route in time to get to the party and draw cartoons for the children. Everyone had a good time, even the clown and balloon man. Darcie took Betty aside and said, "Thank you, Betty, for getting me out of this."

"You're welcome, Darcie," said Betty. "What's the good of helping others all of the time if we can't help each other, too?"

inter**MISSION**

Write two rules that Darcie could follow in the future to keep herself from making promises she can't keep.

1. _____

_____

2. _____

_____

UNIT FOUR
Serving by Sharing Joy

"Rejoice with those who rejoice." Romans 12:15

MEEKNESS ◆ **LOYALTY** ◆ **REVERENCE**

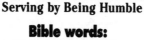

MEEKNESS

Definition:
Serving others with the abilities God has given me.

Opposite:
Showing off with the abilities God has given me.

Serving by Being Humble

Bible words:
"Live in harmony with one another. Do not be proud, but be willing to associate with people of low position. Do not be conceited." Romans 12:16

David's Bout With Conceit

"I'm so excited!" shrieked Darcie. "The people at the senior center will just **love** our program!" The others agreed. The group had enjoyed helping Darcie at the preschool party. Now they wanted to serve the people at the other end of the age ladder.

David was making plans in his head for the solo he hoped to sing. "If I hint around enough, the group will ask me to sing," he thought.

He cleared his throat. "I sang at my church program last spring. Everyone said I did really well." "That's nice," said Betty, turning to Darcie. "How many candy canes are you putting into the Christmas stockings?"

To Henry, David said, "Maybe one of us should sing a Christmas carol alone." "Yeah, maybe," said Henry, watching Jerome. "Jerome, don't get any ideas. This candy is for **people,** not dogs." The dog wagged his tail, hoping that Henry didn't mean it.

David's mouth was open for hint number three when Betty's mother called to him. "David, your mother is here for you." He walked curiously to Betty's front door.

"Hi, David," said his mother. "Dad and I have to go to Grandma's early, so we're picking you up now." David was too logical to argue, so he hollered his goodbyes and headed for the car. All the way to Grandma's, he planned his song.

The next day at school, David found the group and asked about the plans they had made for the program. "Here is a copy of what we decided to do," said Betty.

"Yeah," said Tony, "we knew you would like us to write it out for you. Sorry it's not a print-out." Everyone laughed. David would have laughed, too, if he hadn't just seen the third line of the program. It said: "Solo by Tony." Line eight said, "Lights and mikes handled by David."

David smashed his paper into a ball and threw it into the nearest garbage can. The group watched in shock as he stomped off chewing on the last of some string cheese. "What is wrong with **him**?" asked Tony.

What was wrong was that David was upset because none of his hints worked. "They'll be sorry that I'm not singing instead of him," thought David.

Rehearsals began the next day. David showed up to work the lights and the mikes, but his proud heart was bitter. Betty practiced her cello solo, Darcie told her Christmas story, Henry worked on painting the background scene, and Tony practiced his song. They each tried to talk to David, but he would not talk back to them. No amount of logic could seep through his anger.

After the third practice, Tony caught up with David on his bike. "David, I want to tell you something." David didn't answer. "I want to tell you that I'm sorry you're upset. I'd like to fix whatever is wrong, but I can't do it if I don't know what it is."

"Okay. I'll tell you what is wrong," said David, stopping on the side of the road. "I am a better singer than you are, yet you are the one singing at the Christmas program. I hinted all around that I wanted to do it, but you guys didn't pay any attention to me."

Tony looked surprised. "I didn't know you wanted to sing. I'm sorry." David got back on his bike and headed home at top speed. Tony caught up with him again.

"David," he said, panting, "you're being unreasonable. You're always telling us to think things through, to be logical. Well, take your own ad-vice. You're being conceited and proud and unforgiving." David jerked his head around to look at Tony. "It is not logical to expect people to catch your hints, David. If you want to do something, isn't it **logical** to come right out and say it?"

Tony rode off, leaving David to think about his words. By the next morning, David had worked out his problem. His father had helped him give up his anger and conceit by talking it over between themselves and God. He apologized to the group.

During Tony's song at that day's practice, David was working the mikes and humming along. "That sounds great," said Darcie. "You were harmonizing without even thinking about it!"

Henry overheard Darcie's comment and said, "Maybe David and Tony should sing a duet." The others agreed.

"How do you feel about that, Tony?" asked David.

"Let's try it," he said with a grin. It worked, and the solo became a duet. "I guess I should use my voice for singing, not bragging," said David.

"I won't argue with that logic," laughed Tony.

INTER**MISSION**

Imagine that you are at a planning meeting for a Christmas program. What activity would you most want to do? _____

Keeping meekness in mind, plan a set of words that you could use to let the others know what you want to do. _____

_____

◆ LOYALTY ◆

Serving by Being Faithful

Bible Words:
"For how can I bear to see disaster fall on my people? How can I bear to see the destruction of my family?" Esther 8:6

"Not My Brother!"

Two of Henry's older brothers, Robbie and Matt, were at the grocery store on an errand for their mother. While they were choosing a sack of potatoes, a scowling woman came up to them. "That brother of yours!" she cried. "He's lying to me. He says he has delivered my papers this week, but he hasn't!"

Robbie dropped the sack of potatoes back into the bin and turned to face the angry woman. Before he had a chance to speak, Matt said, "If Henry said he delivered your papers, then he did."

"That's right," added Robbie, "Our brother doesn't lie!"

"Well, he sure did lie to me!" she said.

"Me, too," said another woman nearby. "It's been three days since I've gotten my morning paper."

"Well, something must be happening to them after they are delivered, because our brother would not lie," said Robbie, leaving the potatoes and heading for the door. Matt picked them up and quickly paid for them. After a few minutes, he caught up with Robbie.

"What do you think, Robbie?" asked Matt.

"I don't know, but we're going to find out." The two boys hurried home to find Henry.

What do you think was causing the papers to disappear? Be ready to talk about your idea.

FAMILY LOYALTY

When Queen Esther saw her people in danger, her loyalty caused her to risk her life for them. This kind of loyalty is one of the beautiful parts of being in a family.

Here is a list of other ways people have shown loyalty to someone in their family. *As you read through the list, imagine how it would feel to receive such loyalty.*

A sister donated a kidney to her brother.
A mother stayed up all night with her sick baby.
A father offered to go to prison for his son.
A brother gave blood to help his grandfather.

What acts of loyalty do you know about? _____

_____

_____

LOYALTY TO COUNTRY

During the war in Vietnam, American naval commander, Jeremiah Denton, was shot down by the enemy. They captured him after he parachuted into North Vietnam. The North Vietnamese put him in a terrible prison and treated him very badly. Some days he got nothing to eat, on others just a bowl of thin soup made from the rind of a pumpkin. He became very sick and weak, but no matter what they did he would not answer their questions. He did not want to be disloyal to his country. This made the North Vietnamese very mad. They began to torture Commander Denton in horrible ways. Finally, they did something so painful to him that he promised to answer their questions on a TV show which would be seen in the United States. The North Vietnamese wanted to show how they could make American soldiers confess their "crimes."

The day arrived for the TV interview, and Commander Denton pretended to answer their questions. In America, people watching the show noticed he was blinking a lot. They thought it was due to weakness. But soon they realized he was actually sending morse code by making long or short blinks. The message he sent over and over was – "TORTURE! TORTURE! TORTURE!" When the enemy found out, they were even more angry. They sent him to a prison where his cell was the size of a closet and had no windows. He stayed in that terrible place for many, many months. He prayed a lot and "talked" to other American prisoners by tapping out morse code on the walls with his knuckles.

Finally the day came when the North Vietnamese decided to release the prisoners and let them go back to America. Commander Denton and the other Americans stumbled out of their dark cells into the bright sunlight. They were so weak they could hardly stand, but they linked arms and began to pray and sing hymns. The prison camp commander was furious and ordered his men to stop the singing by beating the Americans with their rifles. When they realized that not even violence would stop the American prisoners, they stepped back and let them finish their joyful meeting. Through more than seven years of imprisonment, Commander Denton had remained loyal to his country. He was so thankful to be going home.

THE LOYAL JESUS

Jesus is loyal. He sticks with us through happy times, sad times, scary times and in-between times.

When Jesus lived on earth, He showed loyalty to those who loved Him. Look up these verses to discover some of the times Jesus showed loyalty.

JESUS REMAINED LOYAL WHEN:

1. Matthew 26:69-75 _____

_____

2. Matthew 26:56b _____

_____

DO YOU?

1. Do you think that these people would be loyal to Jesus if they had another chance? **Yes** _____ **No** _____

2. Do you think a wise person could learn a lesson from the experience of those who were disloyal to Jesus? What would it be? _____

_____

3. Do you think that Jesus still shows loyalty to God's children by speaking up for us when we sin? This is called being our "advocate." Look up the meaning of "advocate" and write it here: _____

_____

_____

Definition:
A deep respect and
awe for someone.

REVERENCE

Serving by Showing the Importance of Others

Opposite:
Not thinking very
highly of someone.

Bible words:
"All the angels were standing around the throne and around the elders and the four living creatures. They fell down on their faces before the throne and worshipped God, saying: 'Amen! Praise and glory and wisdom and thanks and honor and power and strength be to our God for ever and ever. Amen'!" Revelation 7:11, 12

AWE = Aaaahh!

1. When you hear an "aah!" there is often some awe in it. What is the dictionary meaning of awe?

Awe: _____

_____

2. What are some of the reasons a person would say the kind of "aah" with awe in it?

_____

_____

_____

3. In the verse at the top of the page, a group of people are showing awe or reverence. What is happening?

_____

_____

_____

4. Imagine being there! If you have trusted Jesus as the One who did everything that needed doing for you to go to Heaven, then you will see this happen. This verse has been written, but it hasn't happened yet. God is telling us the future.

5. What are five of the millions of reasons that God deserves our reverence? What has He done that makes you say "Aah!"?

1. _____

2. _____

3. _____

4. _____

5. _____

6. We often say "Aah!" about the skills and thrills of athletes, singers, and actors. What has a famous person you admire done to cause you to say "Aah!"?

1. _____
2. _____
3. _____
4. _____
5. _____

7. What are some ways people show that they think a famous person is awesome?

_____

_____

_____

8. Compare your lists in questions 5 and 6.
Which list shows the greatest skills?   #5 _____ #6 _____
Which list deserves the biggest "Aah!"?   #5 _____ #6 _____
Which list usually receives the biggest "Aah!"?   #5 _____ #6 _____

9. Imagine that everyone who has ever lived and loved God is in one place shouting and singing praises to Him. Imagine that everyone who ever denied that God is real is falling in reverence in front of Him. If you have to choose which group to be in, which group would be your choice? Group 1 or Group 2. That is a choice each person must make.

10. In what ways do people show reverence for God today?
- In Betty's church, reverence is shown for God by walking and talking quietly and singing songs with organ music about God's greatness.
- In Tony's church, reverence for God is shown by lively singing and clapping and excited "Amens."

- In your church, reverence for God is shown by _____

_____

11. In what way would you like to show God your reverence, or awe, for Him if He appeared to you

today? _____

_____

Have you ever thought that He might be pleased if you worshipped Him in this way when you are alone? Many people do.

**GOD IS AWESOME
AND
AAH!SOME!**

Esther considers the note that Mordecai sent her about Haman's plan.

ESTHER

News of Haman's wicked plan reached Mordecai. His body shook with sorrow and his soul was overcome with heaviness. "My people are facing death for something that I have done," he cried. Weeping bitterly, Mordecai exchanged his everyday clothes for those made of sackcloth, a scratchy piece of clothing reserved for times of mourning. He poured ashes on his head, which showed everyone the extent of his sorrow. Jews everywhere did similar things to show their own distress.

Mordecai, still dressed in sackcloth and wearing ashes, walked through the town to the palace gate. "I must get in touch with Esther," he thought. No one wearing mourning clothes could enter the palace, so he waited there, believing that Esther would hear about him. When Esther's servants saw her cousin, they told her about his condition. "Take these clothes to him," she said. "He has no reason to do such a thing!" Esther's ears had not yet heard the terrible news.

Mordecai refused to change clothes. Esther knew then that something must have happened. She sent a servant with another message: "What is going on? Why are you mourning?"

Mordecai told the servant everything, even that Haman had wanted to pay the soldiers himself. He gave the servant a copy of the king's decree to give to Esther.

However, Mordecai had more than the news and the decree to give to his cousin, the queen. He had a challenge for her. "Tell Esther to beg the king for mercy and plead with him for her people," he cried. Mordecai was counting on Esther's courage and loyalty to her people to save them.

In the palace, Esther was not feeling courageous. "Go, tell my cousin that everyone here knows that no one just walks in to see the king! I could die if he is not in the mood to see me," she said fearfully.

The servant again met with the wailing Mordecai and spoke Esther's words to him. Through his sorrow, Mordecai said, "Tell the queen these words: Don't think that because you are the queen that your life will be spared. Somehow our people will be delivered; if not by you, then by someone else. But be sure of this, you and I and our family will surely die." Then Mordecai added, "Besides, who is to say that you were not made queen for this very reason?" The servant had written Mordecai's message and quickly took it to the waiting and worried queen.

Esther read the note from her cousin. She had an important choice to make. If she approached the king at the wrong time, she would die. If she didn't approach the king and beg for mercy for her people, she would die anyway. Either way, Esther knew that her life was in danger.

Once again, she sent a message to Mordecai. Mordecai read her note, which said: "Gather our people together and fast for me. Do not eat or drink for three days, night or day. My maids and I will do the same. When the three days are up, I will go into the king even though it is against the law. And, if I die, I die."

Esther had made a choice. Perhaps God did cause her to become queen in order to save His people from death. She chose to show faith. She would serve God and her people with loyalty and courage.

BACK TO BACK FIRE

BACKFIRE 4

1. What did Mordecai do when he found out about Haman's plan?

_____

_____

2. What was Esther's first reaction to finding out about Mordecai's pitiful condition?

_____

_____

3. Why do you think Esther sent a servant to question her cousin? Why didn't she go herself?

_____

_____

4. What was Mordecai's challenge for Esther? Do you think he ever questioned her loyalty to her people?

_____

_____

5. List Esther's arguments for and against what Mordecai wanted her to do. Pretend that you are her most trusted advisor. Write down some of the things you would say to her.

_____

_____

_____

_____

6. Find out what it means to be on the "horns of a dilemma." How was Esther in that condition?

_____

_____

7. Look for any examples of meekness, loyalty, and reverence in the story. Share them with a friend.

UNIT FIVE
Serving by Sharing Sorrow

"Mourn with those who mourn." Romans 12:15

SELF-CONTROL ♦ HONESTY ♦ CAUTIOUSNESS

Definition:
Guarding my life by
making right choices.

SELF-CONTROL

Serving by Restraining Myself From Doing Wrong

Bible words:
"A man of knowledge uses words with restraint, and a man of understanding is even-tempered." Proverbs 17:27

CONTROL CHECK-POINTS

Restraint = to keep under control.
Even-tempered = not quickly angered or excited.

1. Using these definitions and the words from Proverbs 17:27, what would you say a man of knowledge

   would do with his words? _____

   _____

   What would you say is one thing an even-tempered man would be known for? _____

   _____

   _____

   If Tony were to put all of the words he wished he had never spoken into his bedroom, they would
   spill out into the hall. Tony has allowed his temper to bring him some big regrets. Tony, and all of us,
   would be wise to learn to send our words through four check-points before letting them leave our
   mouth.

   The check-points of control are:
      Check-point #1: IS IT TRUE?
      Check-point #2: IS IT THE RIGHT TIME?
      Check-point #3: IS IT FOR THE RIGHT REASON?
      Check-point #4: IS IT HELPFUL?

2. Send each of these examples through the four control check-points. Place a check next to any parts
   that you feel keep it from passing inspection. Make any changes you think are needed by rewriting
   the section that failed inspection.
   a. Betty's friend, Tammy, had invited her to go to summer camp. She was quite sure her parents
      would let her go. Her father had been out of town for three days on an important business trip,
      but the minute he arrived home, Betty said, "Dad, may I go to summer camp with Tammy?"

      Which check-points passed? _____ Which check-points failed? _____

      _____

   b. David liked being the smartest student in computer class. However, he didn't like the way Nathan
      was catching up with him. When David overheard the computer teacher praise Nathan's work to
      another teacher, David felt jealous. The next day, David complimented Nathan on his project, but
      added, "It will be a long time before you know as much as I do, though."

      Which check-points passed? _____ Which check-points failed? _____

      _____

   c. Darcie noticed that Melanie seemed unhappy. She discovered that Melanie and her best friend
      Shawna had been fighting. "If they are still fighting after school, they will spoil the meeting we are
      having about the car wash. I'd better do something about this," she said. When Darcie saw Shawna,
      she said, "Shawna, Melanie wants to see you and say she is sorry." When Darcie saw Melanie, she
      said, "Melanie, Shawna is looking for you. She wants to apologize."

      Which check-points passed? _____ Which check-points failed? _____

      _____

SELF-CONTROL SCAN

1. Search your memory for examples of self-control in the Project Servant stories you have read. Write the examples on these lines: _____

_____

2. Scan the Esther stories. Where is the self-control, and who is showing it? _____

_____

3. Look back over the last three days. Where and when have you seen children or adults stopping themselves before they did wrong? _____

_____

4. Using your memory again, recall these popular Bible stories. Write at least one place in each story where self-control was used or where it was lost.

   a. Samson _____

   b. Annanias and Sapphira _____ _____

   c. Daniel and the three Hebrew boys _____

   _____

   d. Joseph and Potiphar's wife _____

   _____

5. Now run each of these Bible stories through the control check-points. As a story passes a check-mark, place a "+" on the line. As a story fails a check-mark, place a "–" on the line. Be ready to suggest ways the failed check-points could be improved with self-control.

STORY	CHECK-POINTS			
a. Samson	#1: _____	#2: _____	#3: _____	#4: _____
b. Annanias and Sapphira	#1: _____	#2: _____	#3: _____	#4: _____
c. Daniel and the three Hebrew boys	#1: _____	#2: _____	#3: _____	#4: _____
d. Joseph and Potiphar's wife	#1: _____	#2: _____	#3: _____	#4: _____

6. There are many people serving one another with self-control in your city every day. Right now someone is turning in a wallet of money, choosing not to hit someone, telling the truth instead of a lie, or refusing to eat or drink something that would be harmful.

7. How have you served someone recently by being self-controlled? _____

_____

_____

Definition:
Being free of lies.

◆ HONESTY ◆

Opposite:
Being full of lies.

Serving by Being Truthful
Bible words:
"Kings take pleasure in honest lips; they value a man who speaks the truth." Proverbs 16:13

Milk Money Mess-Up

"Darcie, guess what!" shouted Betty. "Mrs. Stoner is going to take the cook's place for a week while she visits her sick mother. Mrs. Stoner has asked us to collect the milk money in her place."

"Oh, good. I **love** handling money," said Darcie. "I'll go tell the others about it."

Mrs. Stoner collected milk money every morning before school began. She would take the thirty cents for a carton of milk, then give each student a milk ticket. The student would give the ticket to the lunchroom clerk and receive a half-pint of milk.

Betty was the first of the group to collect the milk money. She felt pleased with herself as she put each piece of change into the correct section of the money box. "This is easy," she thought.

Things got more difficult when Peter arrived at the ticket table. "Betty," he said with a smirk, "I forgot my milk money today, but I'll bring it tomorrow. Okay?" She stared at him nervously. "Mrs. Stoner lets me do it all the time," he added.

Relieved to hear the loan was nothing new, Betty said, "Well, if Mrs. Stoner does it, then I guess it would be all right." She gave Peter a milk ticket without having any of his money to put in the money box. By the end of her turn, Betty had granted similar favors to four of Peter's friends.

"I hope no one counts the money until Peter and his friends pay back their loans," thought Betty as she walked to the office with the money

box. In spite of what Peter said, Betty was sure he had lied about Mrs. Stoner and the loans. The secretary was on her way out of the office as Betty put the money on the countertop. "Thanks, Betty. Just leave it on my desk. I will count it when I get back."

Fear grabbed Betty's throat. "Maybe I can find five extra tickets in her desk. I could add five more to the box. Miss Montgomery would think that I had sold five tickets less than I really did." As Betty was opening the drawers, the principal walked in.

"Hello, Betty. What are you doing?" he asked.

"Uh, I'm looking for a stapler," she answered.

"The stapler is right here," he said, pointing to the counter.

"Oh, yes. I looked right past it. Thanks," said Betty with a quiver in her voice. She closed the desk drawers and walked toward the stapler. She fumbled for some papers in her backpack. They didn't really need stapling, but she stapled them anyway.

"I'll be right back," said Mr. Simons. "You'd better be getting to class."

"I will, Mr. Simons. Thanks," she said. Then to herself, she thought, "I've got to get to that box. I'll use my lunch money to make up the difference."

Betty was on her way to Miss Montgomery's desk

with the money in her hand when Mr. Palmer, the school counselor, walked through. "Hi, Betty," he said cheerfully. "Why aren't you in class?"

"I'm helping Miss Montgomery," she answered, wondering how she got into this mess.

"Oh, that's nice. How are you helping her?" he asked.

"I'm counting milk money for her," she answered, feeling more than a little scared. She was not used to lying and she didn't like what it did to her.

"Oh. Well, go right ahead. I'm just doing a little work of my own here," he said as he thumbed through some files.

Betty opened the lid of the money box. "Why are you opening the money box, Betty," asked Miss Montgomery as she entered the office.

"Uh, well, I thought I would count it for you," she said, clutching her own money tightly.

"That's not necessary. It only takes me a minute to do it," she said.

Betty turned and walked from the office still holding her money. She needed a place to think, so she stepped inside the broom closet, which was as unusual an idea to her as lying had been.

Ideas for solving her problem came and went through Betty's mind. Most of them were ridiculous. Only one idea stuck. She left the broom closet and headed back to the office. Before she had taken ten steps, Betty was stopped by Miss Montgomery.

"Betty, may I talk to you?" she said.

"I know what you are going to say," said Betty.

"The milk money is $1.50 short. I was coming back to tell you."

"Can you explain it to me?" asked the secretary, lowering her head to look into Betty's eyes.

The weight of her lies lifted as Betty told Miss Montgomery about the loans she had given to Peter and his friends. "They told me that Mrs. Stoner did it all of the time, but later I heard them laughing about how they had tricked me," she said, ashamed. "I thought you wouldn't count the money until the end of the week, and by then I figured I could make them pay it back. I was about to put in $1.50 when you came back into the office."

Miss Montgomery could see that Betty felt very badly about the wrong choices she had made. "Lying gets a little tricky, doesn't it," said the secretary kindly. "It's never worth it, you know. But I'm pleased that you were coming back to tell me about it. I know you are usually an honest girl, Betty."

They walked to the office together. There, Betty admitted her lies to Mr. Simons and Mr. Palmer. They forgave her and said that they would work things out with the boys and the missing money.

When she finally got to her classroom, Darcie said, "Wow, I didn't know collecting milk money took so long! Was it fun, Betty?"

Betty looked at Darcie and said, "Fun? It might have been if I had remembered that I was a money collector and not a loan officer!" Darcie looked puzzled. "Tell you later," said Betty as she reached for her math test. "I hope **these** numbers add up right," she thought with a grin.

INTER**MISSION**

Use your knowledge of the other servant team members to imagine what similar things might have happened to them on the day they collected milk money for Mrs. Stoner.

CAUTIOUSNESS

Serving by Being Aware of Danger and Wrong

Bible words:

"A righteous man is cautious in friendship, but the way of the wicked leads them astray." Proverbs 12:26

Some of God's most helpful words to us are His warnings about the kinds of people to avoid. *Find out who to be cautious of by unscrambling the letters and filling in the correct words on each line. The verse next to each scramble marks the place in the Bible where the warning is given.*

SCRAMBLER

EHT EESSIRAHP __ __ __   __ __ __ __ __ __ __ __ __ __ Matt. 16:12

ETH ETPRUTISTO __ __ __   __ __ __ __ __ __ __ __ __ __ Prov. 7:10, 24, 25

ELPPEO THWI DBA SRETEMP __ __ __ __ __ __ __ __ __ __ __

__ __ __ __ __ __ __ Prov. 22:24

EOELPP HOW LTEL SESTRCE __ __ __ __ __ __ __ __ __ __ __

__ __ __ __ __ __ Prov. 20:19

A HISLOOF NERPSO __   __ __ __ __ __ __ __   __ __ __ __ __ Prov. 14:7

A COMKRE __   __ __ __ __ __ __ Prov. 22:10

53

OTHER WARNINGS

1. What kinds of people do your parents and other leaders warn you about? What are their reasons?

KINDS OF PEOPLE TO AVOID	REASON

2. Circle the entries on your chart that you believe would also be on God's list.

3. Place an "x" by those entries that may not be on God's list, but that you believe He would want you to avoid anyway.

4. Are there any unmarked entries on your list?   **Yes** _____ **No** _____

   What does this tell you? _____

5. Sort out the difference between serving the needs of people and "linking up" with them in friendship. Would the same cautions apply to both?   **Yes** _____ **No** _____ **Why?** _____

6. Jesus spent time with people that the Pharisees called "no goods." What does this tell you about people's opinions of one another?

7. How can a person know whose opinions to take seriously?

8. What help could a verse like Proverbs 13:20 be to someone who is wondering about whom to avoid and befriend?

Be ready to tell about one time a person has kept you from doing wrong, and one time a person has helped you do wrong.

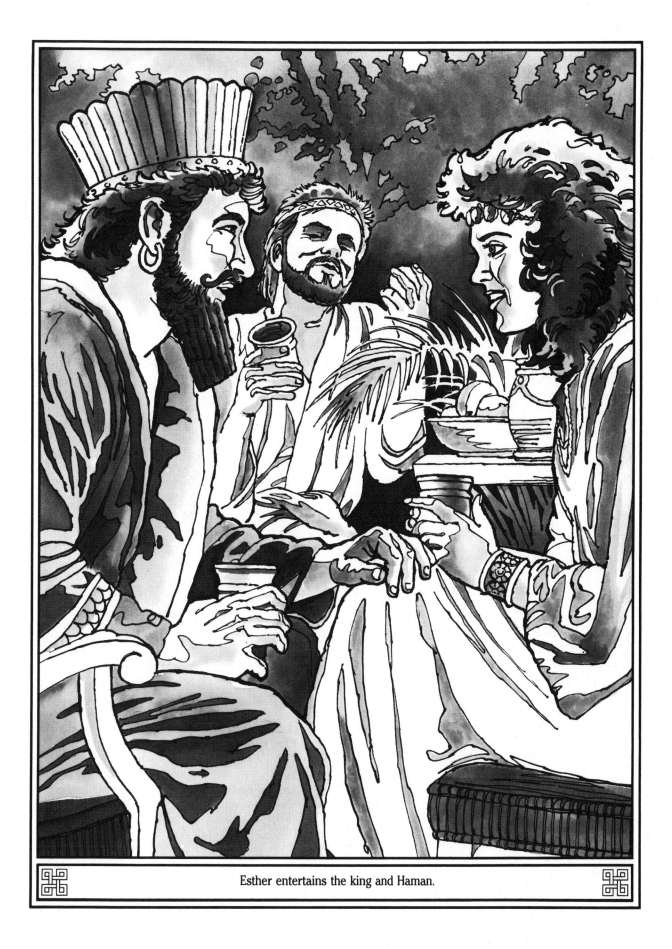

Esther entertains the king and Haman.

BACK FIRE

ESTHER

Stomachs all over the kingdom were raising a fuss. The Jews and Esther had not eaten anything for three days, but no one really cared. After all, they were fasting over an issue of life and death.

On the third day of the fast, Esther kept her promise to Mordecai and the people. She asked her maids to bring out her finest garments and robes. Since she was going to visit the king without being invited, she would look her best. When the time came, she left her part of the palace and walked to the king's court. Her heart was racing within her. "I will know any moment whether I will live or die," she whispered.

She was fearful because she knew that uninvited guests of the king would be killed unless he raised his golden scepter to them. It had been one month since Xerxes had last called for Esther, and she was not sure if her visit would please him.

As Esther stepped into the inner court, the king looked up. She waited, breathlessly, for his response. His face showed pleasure as his hand reached for his scepter. Relieved, but not showing it, the queen stepped forward and touched the tip of the golden sword.

"What is it, Esther," he said, smiling. "What do you want? I'll give you anything up to half of the kingdom."

This is exactly what Esther was hoping he would say. "If it pleases the king," she said, "I would like you and Haman to come to a banquet I have prepared for you."

The king, always ready for a party, sent for Haman, and the two men hurried to Esther's banquet room. The invitation made Haman feel more important than ever before, and he enjoyed every bite and drink of the delicious meal.

After dinner, the king, still curious about the reason behind Esther's visit, said, "Now, Esther. What is it you really want? Remember, I will give you up to half of my kingdom."

Esther spoke her words carefully. "If you view me with favor, and if it pleases you, let the king and Haman come tomorrow to another banquet I will prepare for you. It is then that I will answer your question."

"Very well! We'll be delighted to repeat this wonderful idea," said Xerxes, rubbing his stomach.

Haman held in his screams of joy until he passed through the doors of his own house. He was looking forward to another turn at feeling important. "You'll never guess what happened!" he said to his family and friends. "The queen invited the king and I – just us – to a banquet. I spent all afternoon with them – just us – eating and drinking and talking. Imagine, the king and I and Esther – just us!" He stopped for a quick breath, then continued. "And not only that, but she has invited me **back** for another banquet tomorrow!" Haman's pride was overtaking his mouth and he bragged on and on about himself, his job, his family, and his special friendship with Esther and the king. If Haman had been any more puffed up about himself, he would have been a balloon.

Suddenly, Haman's mind popped his balloon of pride by showing him a picture of Mordecai standing while others bowed to him. "None of these good things really matter to me as long as that Mordecai refuses to honor me!" The memory of Mordecai had caused Haman's joy to fly out the window, leaving him in a cloud of pout.

"Good grief, Haman!" said his wife and friends. "Just build high gallows for the man, get the king's permission to hang Mordecai in the morning, then go to your banquet and have a good time," advised his friends.

"That is a perfectly wonderful idea!" shouted Haman, feeling more cheerful now. "I'll order it done this very minute." Meanwhile, back at the palace, the king was stroking his beard wondering what Esther wanted, and Esther was deep in thought planning the best way to tell him.

BACKFIRE 5

1. How did uninvited visitors to King Xerxes know if they would be received or killed?

_____

_____

2. As Esther stepped into the inner court, how did the king's face reveal his decision about her being there?

_____

_____

3. What was Xerxes' rather amazing offer to Esther? Do you think he was using self-control in making such an incredible offer? How did Esther respond?

_____

_____

4. Can you think of any reason for Esther's strange requests for the king and Haman? Write down some of your ideas.

_____

_____

5. Compare Haman's words and feelings before and after he thought of Mordecai.

_____

_____

6. Haman's wife and friends came up with a great idea to soothe his troubled mind. What was it? Do you think it might wreck Esther's plans?

_____

_____

7. As the king was stroking his beard thinking about Esther, do you think he was feeling cautious about her second banquet and her real wishes?

_____

_____

8. In what ways did Esther display self-control during this episode?

_____

_____

UNIT SIX
Serving by Getting Along With Others

"Live in harmony with one another." Romans 12:16

DILIGENCE ◆ **PATIENCE** ◆ **THOROUGHNESS**

Definition:	DILIGENCE	Opposite:
Doing my work steadily until it is done.	Serving by Finishing What I Start	Quitting when I feel like it.

Bible words:
"Like the coolness of the snow at harvest time is a trustworthy messenger to those who send him;
he refreshes the spirit of his masters." Proverbs 25:13

ERRAND-RUNNING HAZARDS

Being a diligent messenger means overcoming hazards along the way. Darcie has been asked to deliver a message to her mother's best friend who is at the park with her small children. Find the shortest path to the park. Title each hazard in the maze of people and things that you feel might tempt Darcie to stop her errand-running.

IT'S REFRESHING!

1. In a thesaurus find words that mean the same as "refresh." Write them here: _____

   _____

   Circle the word that seems most refreshing to you.

2. God says that you will be these things to those you diligently serve. Name one time you believe you were refreshing to someone you served. _____

   _____

REWARDS OF BEING DILIGENT

3. What awards might a diligent messenger receive? _____

   _____

   Of these, which would bring you the most satisfaction? _____

   _____

MESSAGES

Messages are sent everyday. In ancient times people like the Spartans and Athenians had many messages carried by swift runners who would often brave incredible dangers to accomplish their mission. What kinds of messages do you think these people carried? Did you know that some of the bravest runners died from exhaustion after delivering their message?

What important message did these people send?

a. Esther to Mordecai when she decided to approach the king on behalf of her people.

   _____

   _____

b. Paul Revere to the American patriots.

   _____

   _____

c. Commander Jeremiah Denton when giving a coded message with his eyelids as a prisoner of war.

   _____

   _____

d. The women at the tomb of Jesus.

   _____

   _____

e. Jesus, when he spoke the words in John 3:16.

   _____

   _____

If you choose to be a diligent messenger, you will be joining a group of famous and admired people. You will be a refreshing addition to the world.

Haman leads Mordecai through the streets.

ESTHER

The king's curiosity kept him from sleeping well that night. With every toss and turn of his body, Xerxes tried to guess what favor Esther was going to request. "Maybe she wants me to build her a new library! No. Maybe she wants to take a long vacation!"

When he ran out of ideas about Esther, and was still not asleep, Xerxes woke up his servants. "Read me the record books," he said. The king was sure that the reading of history would put him to sleep. But, like any good history book, it intrigued rather than bored him. Of special interest to him was the part about a man who uncovered a plot to kill the king.

"Has that man Mordecai been rewarded for his loyalty to me?" asked the king.

"No. Nothing has been done for him," answered his attendants.

By this time, the sun was up. Haman was already entering the king's court. He wanted Mordecai to have an early hanging.

When King Xerxes heard someone in the court, he said, "Who is outside?" His servants answered, "Haman."

"Send him in," ordered the king excitedly. Before Haman could say a word, the king began speaking to him. "Haman, what should I do for someone I want to honor?"

"Well," thought Haman, "isn't it grand of the king to want to honor me!" Haman let his imagination carry him to his finest idea. "I suggest that the king honor this person by placing him on one of the king's own royal horses – the kind with the king's crest on it. The honored one should wear a robe that the king himself has worn. Next, one of the king's prized servants should lead the man through the streets of the city shouting, 'This is the man the king wants to honor'!"

Haman was proud of himself for coming up with such a glorious plan. He rubbed his hands together, eager

for his one-man parade to begin. He imagined that he could feel the luxury of the king's robes on his shoulders already.

The king agreed with Haman that his idea was brilliant. "Perfect! Perfect! And that is precisely what I want you to do for Mordecai, the Jew. You know, the one who sits at the palace gate."

Haman's mouth dried up and his cheeks twitched. His breath came out in short puffs, and he shook his head to be sure his ears were working. "I couldn't have heard what I **think** I heard," he thought.

"Hurry up!" said the king. "I want Mordecai to be in my robe and on that horse in less than an hour!"

"It's true, then," mumbled Haman. Rage replaced his shock. Haman slowly realized that Mordecai would be the man honored instead of him and that it would be Mordecai who would be placed upon the king's horse instead of upon Haman's gallows.

Haman walked Mordecai through the streets of the town with legs that felt like lead. Each step added another lump to his throat and another layer to his humiliation. When the ordeal was over and the people of the town knew that the king had honored Mordecai, Haman ran home and covered his head in embarrassment.

His family and friends gathered around him. "Mordecai has started your downfall," they said. "On top of that, he is a **Jew**. There is no way you will stand against him!" Even in their foolishness, Haman's wife and friends were wise enough to know that the God of Israel is more powerful than anyone's wicked schemes.

While his wife and friends were still serving doomish thoughts to Haman, the servants of the king arrived to whisk him away to Esther's second banquet. He was hardly hungry.

BACK TO BACKFIRE

BACKFIRE 6

1. How did King Xerxes try to get to sleep after worrying about Esther's request?

_____

_____

2. What reminded him of his earlier desire to reward Mordecai for loyalty?

_____

_____

3. Draw four pictures of Haman's face. The first should show him waiting outside the king's door, the second should show him listening to what he thought the king was going to do for him, the third should show him at the moment he realized whom the king was really talking about, and the fourth should show him as he led Mordecai around the town.

4. What would have been your recommendation to the king for honoring a person who demonstrated great loyalty?

_____

_____

5. Describe the details of the way in which King Xerxes was going to honor Mordecai.

_____

_____

6. List any parts of this episode that demonstrated initiative, patience, or thoroughness by the characters.

_____

_____

PATIENCE

Serving by Being Gentle

Bible words:
"Be patient, then, brothers, until the Lord's coming. See how the farmer waits for the land to yield its valuable crop and how patient he is for the fall and spring rains. You, too, be patient and stand firm, because the Lord's coming is near." James 5:7, 8

1. Just as the farmer waits patiently for his crops to ripen, we are told to wait patiently for our turn to go to Heaven.

   When Henry was asked to make a list of reasons why he could hardly wait to go to Heaven, this is what he wrote:

   a. God is there waiting to care for me.
   b. I'll get to thank Jesus for dying for my sins.
   c. I'll meet my favorite Bible people.
   d. I'll never have to go to bed.
   e. I'll get to see all of God's best ideas.
   f. I'll be safe from scary people and pain.

   _____

   _____

   _____

2. Add some of your own ideas to Henry's list of reasons.

3. Rank all of the reasons in order of their importance to you.

4. Anticipation means looking forward to something.
   a. Tony anticipated the day he would get to buy a skateboard like the one Travis used.
   b. Betty anticipated the slumber party she was planning for Darcie's birthday.
   c. What have you anticipated? _____

   _____

5. Sometimes the anticipation is more pleasant than the thing we are waiting for.
   a. Tony discovered that he didn't really enjoy skateboarding as much as Travis did.
   b. Betty's slumber party turned into a shouting and pouting party.
   c. How did your anticipation turn out?

   _____

   _____

6. God says that no human mind will ever be able to imagine the wonders of Heaven. This means that no matter how fabulous you think Heaven is, it will be better. Heaven will not be a disappointment. It will be a wonderful surprise.

HEAVENLY TREASURES

In Matthew 6:19-21 Jesus advises us to spend our time building up our treasury in Heaven. This is one wise thing we can do while we wait patiently to go there ourselves.

Knowing what you know of God, what three actions do you believe would build the most treasure in Heaven?

1. _____

2. _____

3. _____

Choose one of the activities and design a Treasury Certificate of Heaven. List the action, state its value, and decorate it in a heavenly way! As you do this, imagine yourself in Heaven opening your treasury vault and finding it full. How can that thought become true? It's up to you.

TREASURY CERTIFICATE
OF HEAVEN

in the amount of

$ _____

awarded to

_____

for

_____.

Date

_____

Definition:
Completing the details
of a task.

THOROUGHNESS

Opposite:
Overlooking the details
of a task.

Serving by Taking Care of Details

Bible words:
"The Lord will fulfill His purpose for me; Your love, O Lord, endures forever –
do not abandon the works of Your hands." Psalm 138:8

932 Messages

Somewhere between the time the Monopoly game began and the moment Tony bought hotels for St. Charles Place, Henry had a good idea. "I think that we should make sure that everyone in our class gets a word of love on Valentine's Day. After all, God loves everybody, and I'm sure He would like us to remind them of it."

Tony stopped counting his money long enough to say, "Okay. Sounds good to me."

"Why just our class?" asked Darcie the following day at school when Henry told her his idea. "Why not both sixth grades?"

"Why not fifth and six grades?" asked Betty at lunch when Darcie told her Henry's idea.

"Why not the whole school?" asked David as he and Betty were walking to choir.

"Why not?" said Henry when he heard how his idea had grown. "I'd like to draw the picture on it, if no one minds." Henry's confidence had grown since last September when he broke his leg.

The time left between Henry's idea and Valentine's Day was only three weeks. "We've got to get going on this or we won't make it," cautioned Tony. They spent the first week gathering names of students and teachers. "I don't believe how hard it is to figure out exactly who is in each class," said Tony. "What if we leave someone out?"

"We won't," said Henry. "You'll see."

The group had decided to print the cards on David's computer using colored paper and fancy type. They would fold the card three times and glue a photocopy of Henry's drawing on the front of each card. "Let's see," said Darcie. "There are 874 kids in our school and 58 teachers. That means that we have to make . . . uh . . . 922 Valentines!"

"No, not 922, Darcie," said David impatiently. "It's 932, which means that each of us is responsible for 187 Valentines."

"186.40 to be exact," said Darcie, hoping to surprise David. "For some reason I never do well in math around him," she thought.

Once the group chose their favorite sketch from the three samples Henry had drawn, they had to decide what to say inside the card. Everyone had a different idea. Two days went by without a decision. On the third day, Tony said, "Let's put the ideas into a bowl and draw one out."

Darcie's slip of paper was drawn from the bowl. David read it out loud, and Darcie said, "I don't like it after all. Let's not use it." They ended up using bits and pieces of everyone's idea for the message inside the cards, but deciding to do that took another day.

"At least we care about what we say on the card," said Henry, looking at the cheery side of things.

"Let's hope that caring doesn't take so long next time," said Tony. "We only have eleven days left."

That afternoon David announced to the group that he had entered the message and the format for the card into the computer. It's ready to print!" Everyone cheered.

The next morning, David didn't want to talk to anyone. It took Betty's special way of caring to find out from him that his father had copied another program over the disk with the Valentine project on it. "He thought it was a blank disk because I hadn't taken the time to put a label on it," said David in a hopeless-sounding way.

The group tried not to groan loud enough for David to hear when Betty passed them the bad news. "Shall we quit this whole thing?" asked Tony.

"Maybe," said Darcie.

"I don't know," said Betty.

"No!" said Henry. "We're not going to let a few little bumps knock us off the road!" The group liked the way Henry used words. "Besides, I just thought of something."

"What?" asked Tony.

"Jesus ran into some giant bumps in the road when He was trying to deliver God's message of love to the world, so why should we let a few little ones stop us," said Henry with excitement. "We can do it. We can. Come on!" He led the group over to David, who gradually left his blues behind and agreed to re-program the message and format on a labelled disk.

On the fifth night before Valentine's Day, another set-back hit the project. "Where's the picture I

left on the coffee table last night," asked Henry in the morning. He heard one "I didn't take it" followed by six "Me neithers." The one member of the family that didn't answer him was the one in the corner sleeping on pieces of shredded paper. Jerome's playfulness had caused another bump in the road.

Tony couldn't believe it when Henry reluctantly told him the upsetting news. "But I'll draw another one tonight," he said.

"Tonight is too late, Henry," said Tony. "I was supposed to take it to the print shop today." The two boys came up with a compromise plan. "You go home right after school and draw another picture and I'll deliver your papers," said Tony. "It'll feel good to do the route again anyway."

Before the boys had a chance to talk about Saturday's game, Betty and Darcie ran up to them and said, "Tony, cross Joey North and Teddy Smith off your list, and, Henry, add Sa Joon Le. The boys are moving to another city and Sa Joon is a new girl from another country." Tony just shook his head. "These bumps are a little too bumpy for me, Henry." The others chuckled at him.

When Valentine's Day arrived and the cards were delivered, Tony decided that the bumps had been worth it. Even his writing hand seemed to hurt less once he saw the cards being read.

"Pretty good idea, Henry," said Tony as he opened his own card. When he read it, he felt as though God Himself was giving him a message of love. "Thanks," he whispered, "for not giving up when the road got bumpy for You."

INTER**MISSION**

Pretend you are as discouraged as David was. What might a caring person like Betty do or say to help you?

UNIT SEVEN
Serving by Accepting People

"Do not be proud, but be willing to associate with people of low position."
Romans 12:16

FORGIVENESS ♦ **FAIRNESS** ♦ **FRIENDSHIP**

Definition:
Caring more about God
than my grudge.

FORGIVENESS

Serving by Giving Up Grudges

Opposite:
Caring more about my
grudge than about God.

Bible words:
"Do not say, 'I'll pay you back for this wrong!' Wait for the Lord, and He will deliver you." Proverbs 20:22

REVENGE!

Taking revenge against someone who has hurt us is a natural feeling. But the child of God has a better way to deal with hurtful feelings. The better way is forgiveness.

Revenge feels good.
Revenge lets me take care of it myself.
God may not take care of it fast enough.
Giving up my grudge seems very difficult.
What harm can a grudge do?

Forgiveness feels better.
Forgiveness lets God take care of it.
But He will always take care of it more lastingly.
It is, unless you give God permission to remove it for you.
It can spoil the sweetness of life.

What is the biggest grudge you can remember holding? _____

_____

If grudges could be weighed on a scale, how much would your grudge have weighed? _____

THINKING THINGS OVER

Think through these questions, then give them your best answers:

1. Who is bothered most by a grudge: the one carrying it or the one it is aimed at? _____

2. Who is helped by a grudge? _____

3. What can a grudge do to help you earn treasure in Heaven? _____

4. What can a grudge do to help you enjoy life while you are living on earth? _____

Answer these questions about forgiveness:

1. Who is helped by forgiveness? _____

2. What can forgiveness do to help you earn treasure in Heaven? _____

3. What can forgiveness do to help you enjoy life while you are living on earth? _____

Absalom – The Grudge Holder

King David did many great things for God. One thing he didn't do very well, however, was be a father to Absalom. Something happened in the king's family that upset Absalom so much that he wanted to kill his step-brother, Amnon.

Amnon deserved punishment, and it is true that David should have given it. Absalom waited two years for his father to punish Amnon. His grudge against Amnon and his father gained weight every day until Absalom's life was one fat and bitter grudge.

After two years, Absalom took things into his own hands. What did his grudge lead him to do? Read about it in

2 Samuel 13:23-29. _____

_____

Imagine that this is a page in David's photo album. Pretend, too, that he is holding a grudge against his neighbor, Jennifer, because she bought the bike she knew he had planned to buy at the corner garage sale.

In each empty snapshot, draw a picture that matches the words underneath it.

This is David and Jennifer at the garage sale.

This is David with his grudge.

This is Jennifer riding the bike she bought at the garage sale.

Here is David watching Jennifer from his bedroom window.

From these pictures, who would you say is suffering the most from the grudge?

David _____ Jennifer _____

If David would give up his grudge and thoughts of revenge, how might God help him?

_____

_____

Haman sprawled across Esther in the banquet room.

ESTHER

BACK FIRE

The ride to the palace was too short for Haman. He needed more time to get himself ready to pretend everything was all right. "How can I sit at a dinner with Xerxes and Esther knowing that Mordecai has just made a fool out of me in front of the entire city!" He tried to comfort himself by thinking ahead to the thirteenth of Adar, the day the Jews would be slaughtered. "At least I will have the last laugh," he thought.

The king waited impatiently for Haman to arrive. He was tired of being curious about Esther's request, and he didn't want to lose another night's sleep over it. When Haman arrived, the two troubled men hurried to Esther's banquet room.

Esther had ordered her maids to fix a meal fit for a king. As they ate, however, none of the three diners tasted much of their food. Their mouths were talking about the weather and politics, but their minds were telling them other things.

The king kept wishing dinner were over so he could ask Esther to name her request. Haman's thoughts raced back and forth between doom and glory, and Esther rehearsed the exact words of her request over and over in her mind.

When dinner was over, the anxious king blurted out his curiosity. "So, Esther, I ask you again. What is it you want? Remember, you may have anything up to half of my kingdom."

Esther changed positions as she readied herself to speak. "This is it," she thought. As she took a deep breath, she could feel her courage mounting. The king leaned toward her, eagerly waiting to hear her words. Haman left his thoughts about Mordecai long enough to copy the interest of the king. Anything that interested the king interested Haman, or so he pretended.

"If I have found favor with the king, and if it pleases your majesty, I plead for my life and the life of my people."

King Xerxes looked confused. Not one of his ideas about her request had even come close to this! He hadn't heard anything about Esther's life being in danger. Haman, on the other hand, was feeling a strange quiver in the pit of his stomach that had nothing to do with the leg of lamb he had just eaten.

"I and my people have been sold to be slaughtered," said Esther. She tried hard to control the pace of her words but they began pushing themselves out quickly. "If we had merely been sold as slaves, I would have kept quiet, because no such distress would have been reason enough to bother you."

By now, Haman's quivering stomach was swirling like an angry sea. "It can't be," he thought. "Esther can't be a Jew! She can't be!"

King Xerxes stood, hoping that by standing he would better understand her words. "Who is the person who has dared to sell your people, Esther?" Then he demanded, "Who is he?"

This was the moment all Israel was waiting for, and it was up to Esther to make it work. Haman was overcome with a dread that seemed to paralyze him. "The man who wants me and my people destroyed is this vile Haman!"

The king was shocked and spun around to look at Haman. It was too much for him to grasp in one moment. He furiously stomped outside to the garden to gather his thoughts. As Haman watched the king head for the garden, there was no doubt in his mind that the king was going to put him to death. His only hope was Esther.

Every piece of pride melted away from Haman.

Nothing mattered to him now except saving his own life. He threw himself across the queen and begged her to save him. At that moment, the king returned to the banquet room. "Oh, I see. I leave you for just a moment and you try to molest my queen!"

"No! No! That isn't it!" cried Haman, but it was too late for words to make a difference. The guards grabbed him and covered his head. On the way out of the room, one of them said, "There is a set of gallows seventy-five feet high at Haman's house. He had them built for Mordecai."

Then, just as his wife and friends had predicted, Haman heard the words of doom. "Hang Haman on those gallows!" When word reached the king that his orders had been carried out, his fury subsided. Xerxes gave all of Haman's land and wealth to Esther, who put Mordecai in charge of it.

Esther's plan had worked, but one problem remained: the king could not take back a decree signed with his ring. Esther had stopped Haman, but now something had to be done to stop the slaughter.

BACKFIRE 7

1. Why did Haman believe that he was going to have the last laugh?

_____

_____

2. Describe Esther's feelings as she prepared to tell the king of her request.

_____

_____

3. What was her request? How did it differ from what the king and Haman thought she was going to ask?

_____

_____

4. Haman obviously didn't do his homework about Esther. What one fact about her background did he overlook, not knowing that it would lead to his death?

_____

_____

5. After Haman realized the deadly peril he was in, he threw himself at the mercy of Esther. If she had had time to consider his sorry state, do you think she would have forgiven him? Do you think she should have forgiven him?

_____

_____

6. One of the qualities of a good king is fairness. Do you think King Xerxes was fair in his punishment of Haman?

_____

_____

FAIRNESS

Serving by Being Impartial

Bible words:
"It is not good to be partial to the wicked or to deprive the innocent of justice." Proverbs 18:5

Kings, queens, and princes used to travel hundreds of miles just to listen to King Solomon judge situations fairly. Many people today wish King Solomon were still alive. They believe that justice is no longer awarded to those who have been unfairly treated.

WORDS TO KNOW ABOUT FAIRNESS

Justice: _____

_____

Guilty: _____

_____

Innocent: _____

_____

Jury: _____

_____

Victim: _____

_____

COURT IN SESSION

If you were on a jury, how would you judge each of these situations fairly? Write your verdict and your opinion about what should be done for the victim and to the person accused of the crime.

CASE 1 A man believes that killing unborn babies is wrong. To try to stop doctors from killing the unborn babies in a small clinic in his hometown, this man chains himself to the clinic door to stop people from entering. He is arrested by the police and charged with criminal trespass and disturbing the peace (he sang hymns while chained to the door).

_____

_____

_____

_____

CASE 2

A family owns several big dogs and keeps them in an area surrounded by a high fence. Some neighborhood children are playing with frisbees when one of the brightly-colored disks flies over the fence. A dog picks it up in its mouth and stands by the fence. One of the children climbs over the fence to retrieve the frisbee and is immediately attacked by several of the other dogs. Before the owners can pull the dogs off, the boy is severely injured and is taken to the hospital. The parents of the boy file a lawsuit against the family that owned the dogs, accusing them of neglecting to post signs warning of the dangerous animals.

_____

_____

_____

_____

 CASE 3

In order to escape from the communists in Russia, a man and his wife hijack a Russian airplane that was headed to Libya. They force the pilot to land at an American airbase in Italy. They are taken into custody by the Americans and flown to the United States, where a grand jury tries to decide whether they should be charged with air piracy.

_____

_____

_____

_____

 CASE 4

A man who has been unemployed for several months is caught by the police taking things from garbage cans without the owners' permission. He is charged with criminal trespass and petty theft. He explains that many people throw away good clothing in their trash that his children could use for the winter months.

_____

_____

_____

_____

 CASE 5

A court has ordered that the children of a broken family should spend half the year with the father and half with the mother. The mother knows that the father likes to have wild parties with drugs and alcohol. She is afraid for the safety of her children when they are with their father. One night a friend calls and warns her of a party that is going on that very evening. She drives over to the father's house and sneaks the children out through the back door. The next morning, when the father finds the children gone, he calls the police and they arrest the mother for kidnapping.

_____

_____

_____

_____

Definition:
Reaching out to others
in a warm-hearted way.

FRIENDLINESS

Serving by Being Kind

Bible words:
"Perfume and incense bring joy to the heart, and the pleasantness of one's friend
springs from his earnest counsel." Proverbs 27:9

Making Friends, Sharing Friends

"Whew!" said Darcie as she wiped her wet forehead. "Mr. Parson gave us a long workout today!"

"What's new," said Monica. Darcie and Monica were on the track relay team. Mr. Parson, their coach, was getting them ready for the city's relay meet at the end of the month.

Darcie was putting her track shoes into her duffle bag when she heard the sound of crying coming from behind the gym lockers. When she poked her head around the corner, she saw Sa Joon crying into a towel.

"Sa Joon," said Darcie, "what's the matter?"

Sa Joon tried to stop her tears, but they came out anyway. Darcie patted her shoulder and wished she knew how to help. "I'll stay here with her until she's better," thought Darcie. Finally, the tears wore out and dried up.

Sa Joon had been a student at Darcie's school for only one month. She was from the country of Korea and was in America with her parents while her father was studying for one semester at the university. She spoke English, but not well enough to be easily understood. All that she said to Darcie was "no friends."

Darcie was the right person to say that to, because she was good at making friends. She coaxed Sa Joon out of the locker room. They walked together to the parking lot where Darcie's mother was waiting for her. At the car, Darcie introduced her mother to Sa Joon.

As Darcie pulled away, she was relieved to see Sa Joon wave to her. "We'll just have to make sure that 'no friends' turns to 'many friends,'" she thought.

Arrangements were made for Sa Joon to visit the Carlisle home the following Friday. At dinner, Darcie's two older brothers got the family laughing when they tried to see who could pile the most peas onto a dinner knife. Sa Joon laughed, too, and seemed glad to be there.

After dinner, the girls went into Darcie's bedroom. She had a stuffed animal collection that covered the bed and filled the shelves. Sa Joon looked at each one carefully, obviously enjoying the cloth zoo. She especially seemed to like a small snuggly bear with a heart sewn onto his chest.

"You can take him home for awhile, if you want to, Sa Joon," said Darcie, holding the bear out to her new friend. Sa Joon said, "No, no. Your bear, not mine."

Darcie tried again and said, "We'll share the bear." She moved her hand out and back as she spoke, hoping the gesture would explain the message. Sa Joon understood and shyly took the bear.

Darcie was good at having fun with friends. She had learned that it was easier to have fun with someone if you did things together. So Darcie's job became one of finding things for Sa Joon to do and locating people with whom to do them. She spent the next few days doing just that.

"That's right. Now press this button to clear the screen," said David to Sa Joon. He was teaching her how to use the computer as a favor to Darcie. It turned out to be a favor to him, too, because by helping Sa Joon learn to use the computer, he came up with a program idea that would help kids learn to speak English. "I'm going to enter the program into the contest at the computer store downtown," he said after the lesson. He wasn't sure Sa Joon understood all of that, but he knew she would soon enough. At school, David and Sa Joon would look at computer books and ads in magazines. One day she left Darcie in the middle of a sentence to go look at the new office computer with David. Darcie couldn't decide whether to be sad or glad.

In the meantime, Sa Joon was also learning how to cook American food. Betty had agreed to give her four cooking lessons. The two girls had a great time in Betty's kitchen cooking hamburgers, fried chicken, tacos, and apple pie. It was so much fun that they decided to have Sa Joon teach Betty to cook Korean food. Darcie was happy that things were going so well, but once in a while she felt left out and a little jealous.

On two Saturdays in a row, Tony taught Sa Joon how to play a basic game of basketball. "She's a natural, Darcie," he said when Darcie walked onto the outdoor court.

"Yes, I know. Coach Parson has asked her to be on the relay team for the meet next week," said Darcie.

Henry was reluctant to become friends with Sa Joon. It wasn't that he didn't like her or want to be friendly; it was that he was shy. In a moment of courage, he told Darcie that he would like to teach Sa Joon how to get around town on her bike.

"That's great, Henry," said Darcie. They talked it over with Sa Joon and set a time for their tour on bikes. Darcie was hoping that they would invite her to go along, but they didn't think of it.

That night in her room, Darcie sat among her stuffed animals feeling lonely. Her mother came in to show her the gift she had bought for her aunt's birthday, but Darcie hardly even looked at it.

"What's up, sweetie?" asked her mother. "You look like you've lost your best friend." Her mom said that nearly every time Darcie looked sad, but this time it was true. Or at least she felt like it was. Darcie began to cry like Sa Joon had done that day in the locker room.

Mom comforted her and listened to her tell how she had helped Sa Joon find new friends. "But now I feel like they like her better than they like me," she said.

Mom understood and said, "Darcie, I just want to say one little thing. It is important to make friends but it is also important to share them." She hugged her daughter and left the room to let Darcie think about things.

Darcie thought, "I guess that I can be greedy about my friends and lose them or be generous with them and keep them." She turned over on her bed and looked her stuffed dog in the eye. "Sounds simple enough. I choose to keep them."

The next day, Sa Joon asked Darcie to come over to her house after school. When Darcie entered the house, Sa Joon led her into the kitchen where, on the table, was a cake and a card. Sa Joon had made the cake herself, and the card had been designed and printed on the computer. The cake said, "To my friend." The card said, "Dear Darcie, You have taken me from no friends to many friends. I am happy here now. May I be your good friend forever? Love, Sa Joon."

Darcie said, "Yes, you can be my good friend forever." To herself she said, "Making friends is fun, but keeping them is more fun."

INTER**MISSION**

If you were one of Darcie's friends, what might she have asked you to teach Sa Joon? What do you wish someone would teach you to do?

UNIT EIGHT
Serving by Being Humble

"Do not be conceited." Romans 12:16

INITIATIVE ♦ LOVE ♦ BOLDNESS

INITIATIVE

Definition:
Carrying an idea from
my mind into reality.

Opposite:
Letting others get
things started.

Serving by Being Inventive

Bible words:
"Do not merely listen to the word, and so deceive yourselves. Do what it says." James 1:22

Friends Forever

On their next bike ride, Sa Joon, or "Saj" as the group liked to call her, invited Henry to go with her family to the zoo the following Sunday. "Thanks, but I go to church on Sundays," he said.

"Oh, yes, I forgot," she said. "I've never been to church."

"Never?" asked Henry.

"Not really, just to . . . what you call them . . . uh . . . funerals," she said. "What is so good about church, Henry?"

"It's that I go there to worship God, the One who made the universe and everything in it," he said.

"I see." She sped ahead of him. "Well, sorry you can't go to the zoo." She had reached her turn-off and was waving goodbye to Henry. He waved back.

The next day at school, while Henry was shooting hoops with Tony, he mentioned his talk with Saj about church. "You mean she's not a Christian?" asked Tony. "Why is she going to a Christian school, then?"

Henry laughed. "Come on, Bounce, you know that everybody who goes to this school isn't a Christian." Tony liked it when people called him by his nickname.

"Yeah, I guess you're right," said Tony.

When Betty and Darcie heard that Saj had never been to church, they said, "So Henry, why don't you invite her to your church?"

"Well, I thought about it, but I wasn't sure she would want to go," he said.

"It doesn't matter if she goes with you," said David. "What matters is that you invited her."

The next time Henry saw Saj, he said, "I was wondering if you would like to come to church with me some Sunday."

"I don't know. I'll have to think about it," she said. Henry's heart was beating quickly. It wasn't used to his boldness.

At lunch, David said, "Why are you making such a big deal about talking to someone about God?" The group could feel one of David's logical speeches coming on. "After all, God is the most powerful Being in the universe, and He loves us. Why **not** talk about Him? We talk about our parents and our friends and our vacation plans to people, so why not talk about God in the same way? I just don't get it." David had a way of explaining things so that people could understand them.

Betty said, "I think David's right, and I want to try talking about God in the same way I talk about other things. I'm going to start doing that today."

"Me, too," said Darcie. David and Henry joined in, too. Tony was quiet, and he left the lunch table early.

On the bus ride home, Betty sat next to Sandra, a fifth grader. They saw a rainbow in the sky and Betty said, "Just think! We are loved by the God who makes those."

After school, Darcie carried two grocery bags home from the store for her neighbor, Mrs. Werlie. The lady was so glad for the help that she gave Darcie a pint of strawberry freezer jam she had made that morning. Darcie thanked her and said, "Isn't it nice of God to make strawberries?" Mrs. Werlie agreed.

David spoke of God to the mailman. He had gotten some letters mixed up and needed to make a special trip back to David's block. "I'm not having such a good day," he said.

"That's too bad," said David. "At least it's good to know that God loves you."

The next day each person reported to the others. They were excited. "This is great," said Betty. "What did you do, Tony?" she asked. Tony just shook his head and looked away.

A few days later, the group and Saj were eating apples under the tree in Darcie's yard. "These are so good," said Saj.

"Yes. Who would ever guess that they were the cause of such trouble," said Darcie.

"What trouble," asked Saj.

"They weren't the **cause** of any trouble," said David. "They were part of the problem. And no one knows for sure that it was an apple that they ate, Darcie."

Saj looked confused and asked, "**What** are you talking about?" The group let David explain.

"Well, when God created Adam and Eve, the world was a perfect place. God would walk with them in their garden home. They would live forever as long as they didn't eat the fruit of one certain tree."

"What tree was that? And why couldn't they eat from it," asked Saj.

"The fruit of this tree was more than just tasty; it was powerful. With a single swallow, they would be given the ability to do right **and** wrong. Once they could do wrong, or sin, their life in the garden and their friendship with God would end."

"**And**," said Darcie, "the sin would pass on to their children and their children's children until it reached everyone who would ever be born."

"Except One," said Henry.

"Anyway," said David, eager to get to the good part of the story, "it was God's enemy, Satan, who got them to disobey God and eat the fruit. He wanted to spoil God's plan for man because He hates God and wants to be in charge."

"One of God's rules is that when sin is committed, someone's blood must be shed. He loved Adam and Eve yet He had to obey His own rule. So, he killed two lambs in their place."

"Then, one day, God came to earth Himself wearing the body of a person. His name was Jesus, and He chose to die in our place, just like those little lambs."

"He did?" asked Saj. "Your God did that?"

Henry shook his head and said, "Yes, He did. And then He came back to life and returned to Heaven. He's there now getting it ready for anyone who believes that He died in their place."

"He's saving a spot for me," said Darcie.

"Me, too," said David.

"Me, three," said Betty.

"Me, four," said Henry.

Tony said, "Not me." Everyone stared at him in unbelief. "But I'd like Him to save me a place."

"Me, too," said Saj.

And there, under the apple tree, two more reservations were made for Heaven. "Now we're **really** forever friends," said Darcie.

INTER**MISSION**

David explained God's plan of salvation in the way he liked best. If you had been under the apple tree that day, how would you have explained it? Write your ideas on a separate piece of paper.

Definition:
Caring strongly for a
person or thing.

LOVE

Serving by Being Unselfish

Opposite:
Not caring about a
person or thing.

Bible words:
"Above all, love each other deeply, because love covers over a multitude of sins." I Peter 4:8

COMMAND CENTER

God is eager for His family to love each other deeply. In fact, of all the things
He tells us to do for one another, loving each other is tops.
Select six verses from the pool of verses at the bottom of the page.
Fit them into the command center in the order you believe they belong.

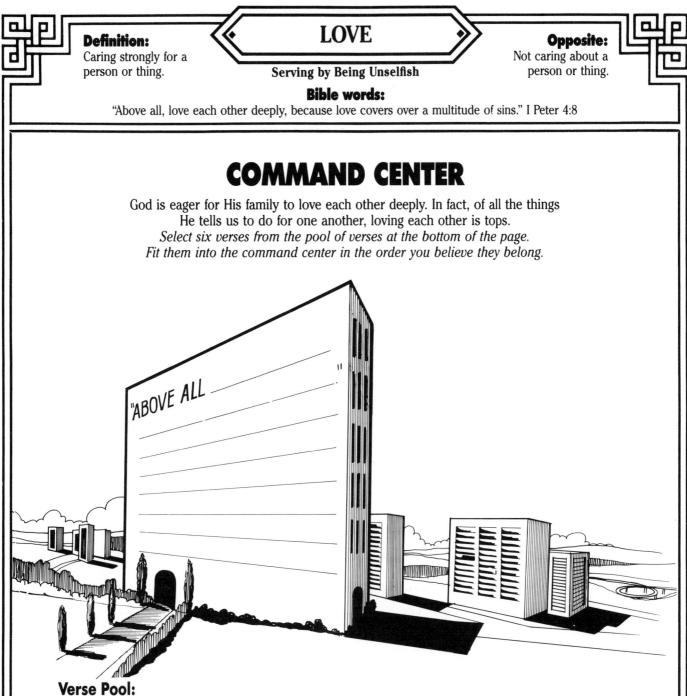

"ABOVE ALL

Verse Pool:

Ephesians 6:7: "Serve wholeheartedly, as if you were serving the Lord, not men."

Philippians 2:3: "Do nothing out of selfish ambition or vain conceit, but in humility consider others better than yourselves."

Matthew 18:15: "If your brother sins against you, go and show him his fault, just between the two of you."

Ephesians 5:19: "Speak to one another with psalms, hymns and spiritual songs."

Luke 6:35: "But love your enemies, do good to them, and lend to them without expecting to get anything back."

I Corinthians 10:24: "Nobody should seek his own good, but the good of others."

Ephesians 5:21: "Submit to one another out of reverence for Christ."

Ephesians 4:32: "Be kind and compassionate to one another, forgiving each other, just as in Christ God forgave you."

LOVING WITH THE LOVE OF JESUS

There is love, and then there is **love**. The finest kind of love is the kind that comes straight from the heart of Jesus. He sends it through God's children to the people that He wants to love, which is everyone.

NATURAL AND SUPERNATURAL

It is **natural** for us to hate.
It is **supernatural**, or not natural, for us to love unselfishly.

LOVE IS A CHOICE

The child of God must make a choice: Shall I let the love of Jesus pass through me or shall I plug it up?

HOW TO RECOGNIZE THE LOVE OF JESUS

A person can recognize the love of Jesus because it does unexpected things. That shouldn't surprise us because when Jesus lived on earth, He loved in unexpected ways. **Think of three ways Jesus loved in unexpected ways and tell them to a friend in class.**

Read each of the situations listed below. On the lines next to the situations, write ways the love of Jesus might unexpectedly show itself through another person.

THE SUPERNATURAL LOVE OF JESUS

THE SITUATION	THE LOVE
1. David's brother erased one of David's diskettes.	_____ _____ _____
2. A player purposely elbowed Tony and called him "Jerk."	_____ _____ _____
3. One of Henry's customers accused him of stealing the milk money left on his porch.	_____ _____ _____
4. Betty discovered that a girl who hated her was very ill.	_____ _____ _____
5. Darcie's mother was upset about something at work. Her distress caused her to yell at Darcie for no reason.	_____ _____ _____

The love of Jesus passes through God's children whose hearts are turned toward Him in love and obedience.

Definition:
Facing life in a daring way.

◆ **BOLDNESS** ◆

Serving by Being Courageous

Opposite:
Facing life in a cowardly way.

Bible words:
"When I called, You answered me; You made me bold and stouthearted." Psalm 138:3

SERVING GOD BOLDLY

At this very moment, there are people all over the earth who are boldly serving God. One person who boldly served God while he lived on earth was King David.

1. David wrote the words to Psalm 138. Read the words he wrote in verse three which is at the top of the page.

   What did God do when David called to Him? _____

   _____

   What did God do for David? _____

   _____

2. David gives credit to God for his boldness. There are many bold ways David served God. In fact, the stories of David's life are very exciting.

Look up these verses, then cross out the parts of his life that are NOT mentioned in them.

I Samuel 16:13
I Samuel 19:2
I Samuel 20:17
2 Samuel 5:4
2 Samuel 6:14

BOLD FACTS ABOUT DAVID'S LIFE

Annointed king of Israel.

Killed Goliath while a young man.

Pursued by King Saul.

Enjoyed a special friendship with Jonathan, Saul's son.

Spared Saul's life when he could have taken it.

Sorrowed over the deaths of Saul and Jonathan.

Took over the throne as king.

Returned the Ark of the Lord back to Israel.

Pursued by his own son, Absalom.

From magazines and newspapers, select pictures of people serving one another with boldness. A picture of a fireman fighting a fire, for example, would show boldness.

Follow your teacher's instructions about collecting and mounting the pictures on this page.

LIVING BOLDLY

Esther and Mordecai celebrate God's deliverance.

ESTHER

BACK FIRE

Following Haman's hanging, Esther told the curious king all of the details surrounding Haman's terrible plot. She explained that she and Mordecai were cousins and that she, too, was a Jew. The story stirred the king.

Esther fell weeping at his feet. She begged the king to show mercy to her people. He held out his golden sceptor, giving her permission to stand and discuss the matter.

"If it pleases the king, make a second decree overruling the one Haman wrote," she cried. "I can't bear to see disaster fall on my people."

"Write another decree in any way you wish," said the king, "and seal it with this." He handed his ring to Mordecai, the same ring that had been on Haman's hand earlier in the day.

Once outside the king's court, Esther and Mordecai grabbed one another in a joy-filled hug. They had difficulty finding words to express their happiness over what God was doing through them.

Esther and Mordecai wasted no time in calling for the secretaries. Because a decree signed with the king's ring could not be reversed, the two cousins had to come up with a way of working around the first one. Their wise plan was this: they would grant permission from the king for all Jews to defend themselves from their enemies on the thirteenth of Adar.

The secretaries wrote out the decree in the language of every province. The news was delivered by messengers on galloping palace horses and was posted in public places by province officials. The cries of happy Jews blended into one giant shout of praise to their God.

Once the decree was written, Mordecai left the palace. He had discarded his mourning clothes and was now wearing glorious garments of blue and purple. On his head was a royal crown, and his hand displayed the king's own ring.

Word spread quickly among those who were not Jews. They became afraid, and many became Jews because they were afraid not to be. The God of the Jews did

awesome things, and they didn't want to be caught on the side of His enemies.

As the months passed, the Jews – and those who planned to kill them – prepared for the attack. All of the officials in the provinces had turned to the side of the Jews. They were afraid of Mordecai because they knew that God was on his side. Mordecai's power increased every day.

Finally, the thirteenth of Adar arrived. Haman's loyal troops began their attack but were soundly slaughtered by the Jews. Haman's ten sons were also killed. At the end of the day, the king brought the battle report to Esther and asked her if there was any other wish she wanted granted.

"If it pleases the king, give the Jews in Susa one more day to continue the battle, and let us hang Haman's ten sons from poles in the city." The king commanded that this be done. So, the Jews in Susa completed their defense in two days. Those living in the country did the job in one. Everyone stopped to celebrate on the following day. They gave gifts to one another and rejoiced in their God.

Mordecai sent letters to all of them asking them to set aside the fourteenth and fifteenth of Adar every year for a holiday. "Stop what you are doing to celebrate this day as the time when the Jews got relief from their enemies," he wrote. "Remember that on this day our sorrow was turned to joy and our mourning was changed to celebration." He then instructed them to give gifts to the poor as part of their activities. He named this holiday "Purim," because Haman had cast lots, or "pur," to choose the day of the slaughter.

Following the battles and the celebrations, things in the palace settled back into a royal pace. Xerxes remained an easy-going king. Esther continued to serve Xerxes as king and her God as Lord. Mordecai took over Haman's position as second in command. He was well-loved by the people because he cared about them and found ways of working for their good.

And so ends the story of history's loudest backfire.

BACK TO BACKFIRE

BACKFIRE 8

1. How did the king show mercy to Esther after she fell weeping at his feet?

   _____

   _____

2. How did Mordecai and Esther display initiative in solving the problem of the original decree?

   _____

   _____

3. Describe the sequence of events leading up to the Jews' victory over their enemies in Susa and in the countryside.

   _____

   _____

4. What did Mordecai tell the Jews to do to express their joy over their victory and their love for God?

   _____

   _____

5. Think of the relationships described at the end of the story between Esther, King Xerxes, Mordecai, and the Lord. A diagram of our own government in America might look like this:

   PRESIDENT
   ↓
   VICE-PRESIDENT
   ↓
   CONGRESS
   ↓
   THE PEOPLE

   Draw a similar chart showing what the government of King Xerxes might look like (be sure to include Esther, the king, Mordecai, and God). Compare your finished diagram with others in the class. In what position did you put God?

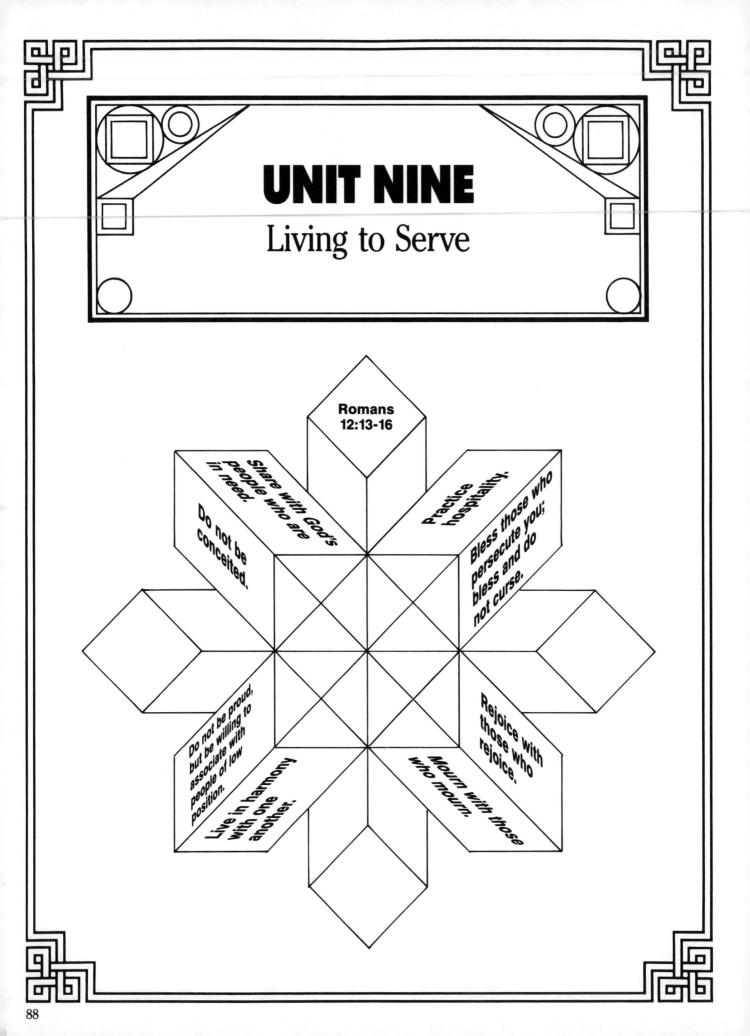

UNIT NINE
Living to Serve

Romans 12:13-16

Share with God's people who are in need.

Practice hospitality.

Do not be conceited.

Bless those who persecute you; bless and do not curse.

Do not be proud, but be willing to associate with people of low position.

Rejoice with those who rejoice.

Live in harmony with one another.

Mourn with those who mourn.

SUMMER PLANS

When it came time for school to end, the group had mixed feelings. Before school had started in September, they hardly knew each other. Now they were best friends.

What began as a way to help one person, ended as help to lots of people. "This servant stuff is okay," said Tony. "Of course, that's because it's the Jesus way of living." Tony was enjoying being a child of God.

They agreed to send and receive messages at the little grocery store near the school. Mr. Friesen, the store owner, agreed to let them keep a clipboard at the register for messages.

1. At the end of summer, what do you think the clipboard looked like? Write your idea on a separate sheet of paper.

2. What do you think each member of the group did during the summer?

   _____

   _____

   _____

   _____

   _____

3. If David were asked what the group learned about serving others this year, what do you think he would say?

   _____

   _____

   _____

4. Using your memory, recall ways that each member of the group served in the stories.

   Tony _____

   Darcie _____

   David _____

   Betty _____

   Henry _____

   _____ _____
   Your Name

5. Write your name on the last line of the list. Recall ways that you served others this year.

Look through magazines and catalogs until you find five pictures of people whom you think most closely match your idea of the kids on the servant team. Label each picture.

THE SERVANT TEAM

Tony "Bounce" Erving ★ David "Doc" Peterson ★ Elizabeth "Betty" Canterbury
Darcie Carlisle ★ Henry "Klink" Klinkdale (and Jerome!)

Thinking back on Backfire!

THINKING BACK ON BACKFIRE

*You have been reading about Esther for several months. Now it is your turn to put some of **your** thoughts on paper!*

1. What could a person learn about God from the story of Esther?

_____

_____

2. What could a person learn about serving God from the story of Esther?

_____

_____

About serving others? _____

_____

3. Describe in complete sentences the sights and sounds you might have seen and heard if you had been:

a. The horse upon which Mordecai rode the day Haman led him through the streets with full honors.

_____

_____

_____

b. A secretary in a meeting with Persian officials the day they received word of the king's second decree granting the Jews permission to defend themselves against the slaughter. _____

_____

_____

_____

c. The palace kitten on Esther's lounge chair the moment she exposed Haman's plot. _____

_____

_____

_____

d. A Jewish child whose mother had just received the news of Haman's plan to kill all of your people, including you. _____

_____

_____

_____

THE KIND OF SERVANT I WANT TO BE

Use these lines to deposit your thoughts about the kind of servant you would like to be to God and others. (1) Name specific acts of service you dream of performing. (2) List two or three reasons you want to do them; (3) Write a paragraph as if someone were writing about you and your life ten years from now.

MY DREAMS OF SERVICE

_____

_____

_____

_____

_____

_____

_____

_____

REASONS I WANT TO SERVE IN THESE WAYS

_____

_____

_____

_____

_____

_____

_____

_____

_____

THE LIFE AND SERVICE OF _____ **IN 19** ____

_____

_____

_____

_____

_____

_____

_____

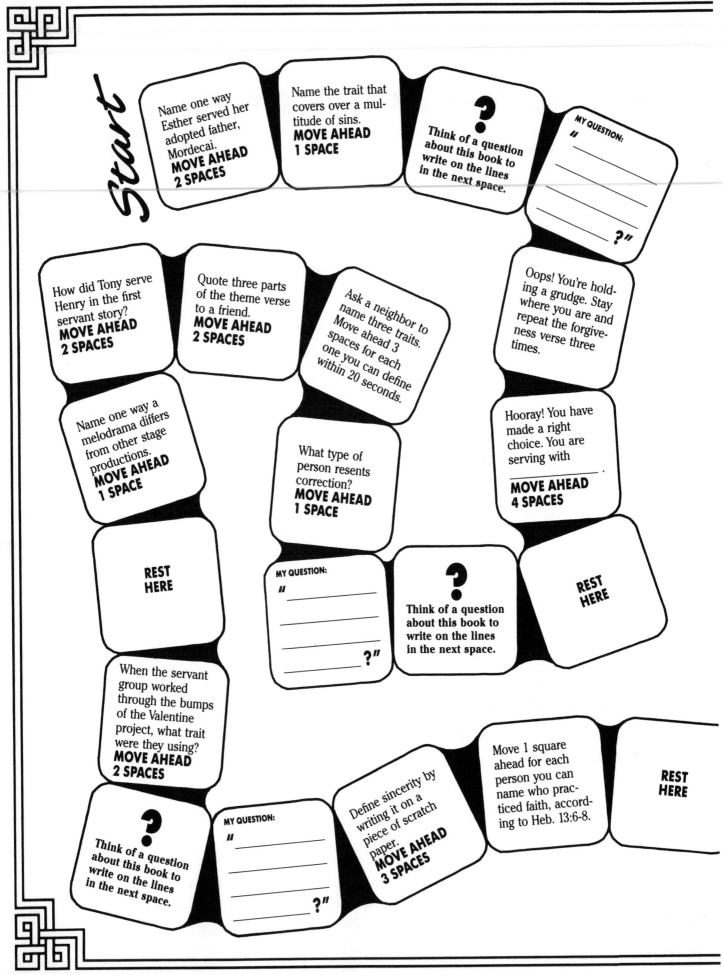

Start

Name one way Esther served her adopted father, Mordecai. **MOVE AHEAD 2 SPACES**

Name the trait that covers over a multitude of sins. **MOVE AHEAD 1 SPACE**

? Think of a question about this book to write on the lines in the next space.

MY QUESTION:
" _____
_____
_____
?"

How did Tony serve Henry in the first servant story? **MOVE AHEAD 2 SPACES**

Quote three parts of the theme verse to a friend. **MOVE AHEAD 2 SPACES**

Ask a neighbor to name three traits. Move ahead 3 spaces for each one you can define within 20 seconds.

Oops! You're holding a grudge. Stay where you are and repeat the forgiveness verse three times.

Name one way a melodrama differs from other stage productions. **MOVE AHEAD 1 SPACE**

What type of person resents correction? **MOVE AHEAD 1 SPACE**

Hooray! You have made a right choice. You are serving with _____. **MOVE AHEAD 4 SPACES**

REST HERE

MY QUESTION:
" _____
_____
_____
?"

? Think of a question about this book to write on the lines in the next space.

REST HERE

When the servant group worked through the bumps of the Valentine project, what trait were they using? **MOVE AHEAD 2 SPACES**

? Think of a question about this book to write on the lines in the next space.

MY QUESTION:
" _____
_____
_____
?"

Define sincerity by writing it on a piece of scratch paper. **MOVE AHEAD 3 SPACES**

Move 1 square ahead for each person you can name who practiced faith, according to Heb. 13:6-8.

REST HERE

Sorry. You were overheard bragging. **GO BACK 1 SPACE**

Congratulations! You are on time, which means that you are _____ . **MOVE AHEAD 1 SPACE**

? Think of a question about this book to write on the lines in the next space.

MY QUESTION: " _____ _____ _____ ?"

In the punctuality verse, what word names a lazy person? **MOVE AHEAD 1 SPACE**

REST HERE

Quote the definition of fairness to your neighbor. **MOVE AHEAD 3 SPACES**

After planning how you will serve your teacher before school ends, move ahead 2 spaces.

How did Betty serve Darcie at the preschool? **MOVE AHEAD 1 SPACE**

Take a bow! Your project to raise money for new library books was a success. You showed _____ . **MOVE AHEAD 2 SPACES**

Listen to advice and accept what to become wise? **MOVE AHEAD 1 SPACE**

You lost patience. **GO BACK 2 SPACES**

Spell the name of the king in the Esther story and move ahead 1 space.

? Think of a question about this book to write on the lines in the next space.

MY QUESTION: " _____ _____ _____ ?"

REST HERE

Move one space ahead for each time you were bold for the Lord this week.

What can a child of God do that Esther couldn't do in the king's court? **MOVE AHEAD 2 SPACES**

Jesus deserves my trust because He is the same _____ , _____ , and _____ . **MOVE AHEAD 1 SPACE TO WIN!**

Finish

95